FREUD'S CLINICAL DEVELOPMENT

FREUD'S CLINICAL DEVELOPMENT

METHOD—DATA—THEORY

Donald Meltzer

THE HARRIS MELTZER TRUST

Freud's Clinical Development first published in 1978 by Clunie Press for
The Roland Harris Educational Trust
Combined edition of *Freud's Clinical Development, Richard Week-by-Week,*
and *The Clinical Significance of the Work of Bion* published in 1998 by Karnac Books
as *The Kleinian Development.* Reprinted in 2008 for The Harris Meltzer Trust.
New edition 2018 by The Harris Meltzer Trust
60 New Caledonian Wharf
London SE16 7TW

British Library Cataloguing in Publication Data
A C.I.P. for this book is available from the British Library

   ISBN 978 1 912567 42 3

Edited, designed and produced by The Bourne Studios
www.bournestudios.co.uk
Printed in Great Britain

www.harris-meltzer-trust.org.uk

CONTENTS

Donald Meltzer (1923–2004) was born in New York and studied medicine at Yale. After practising as a psychiatrist specialising in children and families, he moved to England to have analysis with Melanie Klein in the 1950s, and for some years was a training analyst with the British Society. He worked with both adults and children, and was innovative in the treatment of autistic children; in the treatment of children he worked closely with Esther Bick and Martha Harris whom he later married. He taught child psychiatry and psychoanalytic history at the Tavistock Clinic. He also took a special scholarly interest in art and aesthetics, based on a lifelong love of art. Meltzer taught widely and regularly in many countries, in Europe, Scandinavia, and North and South America, and his books have been published in many languages and continue to be increasingly influential in the teaching of psychoanalysis.

His first book, *The Psychoanalytical Process,* was published by Heinemann in 1967 and was received with some suspicion (like all his books) by the psychoanalytic establishment. Subsequent books were published by Clunie Press for the Roland Harris Educational Trust which he set up together with Martha Harris (now the Harris Meltzer Trust). The *Process* was followed by *Sexual States of Mind* in 1973, *Explorations in Autism* in 1975 (with contributions from John Bremner, Shirley Hoxter, Doreen Weddell and Isca Wittenberg); *The Kleinian Development* in 1978 (his lectures on Freud, Klein and Bion given to students at the Tavistock); *Dream Life* in 1984; *The Apprehension of Beauty* in 1988 (with Meg Harris Williams); and *The Claustrum* in 1992. *The Educational Role of the Family: A Psychoanalytical Model* (commissioned for the OECD with Martha Harris) and first published in French in 1976; a new English edition was published in 2013. As a result of his worldwide teaching several compilations exist of his supervision seminars, including *Meltzer in Barcelona* (2002), *Meltzer in Venice* (2016), *Meltzer in Sao Paulo* (2017), and *Meltzer in Paris* (2017). Other accounts by some who use his work in their own teaching practice are in *Teaching Meltzer* (2015). An introductory selection from his writings may be found in *A Meltzer Reader* (2012) and sample papers on the HMT website www.harris-meltzer-trust.org.uk.

Meltzer describes the series of lectures on Freud, Klein and Bion known as *The Kleinian Development* as both a quest for personal integration into some kind of 'combined internal psychoanalytic object', under whose aegis he personally could aspire to work, and as a vademecum for students. They were originally delivered to students at the Institute and at the Tavistock, specifically with the aim of demonstrating the logical development of that line of psycho-analytic practice. Seeking for this logical development reveals 'an unfolding of method, leading to discovery of new realms of phenomena, generating in turn new models of the mind, which then modify method, etc.'

The lectures on Freud therefore are concerned less with his theory of mind and more with the spiralling alternation of thinking and clinical discovery. Meltzer focuses on those papers, mainly clinical, which highlight key moments of change in Freud's own knowledge and understanding, brought about by the impact of what Bion was to call 'learning from experience' with its inbuilt autobiographical implication. These include: the 'Fragment' on Dora in which Freud's curiosity (about the new method) enabled him to press on where Breuer had retired after his experience with with Anna O. (the 'inventor of psychoanalysis'); the work with Little Hans which established the significance of childhood but only retrospectively; the new evidence of internal conflict manifest by the Rat Man; the Leonardo paper, not for its initiation of the 'bad tradition' of psychobiography but for its autobiographical examination of the ideas of sublimation and narcissisim; the Schreber memoir in which Freud began to conceptualise the reality of the inner world; the 'child being beaten' which demanded a new understanding of masochism; and the Wolf Man with its central phantasy of the primal scene, and the idea of true bisexuality (rather than active-passive trends) and the 'complete Oedipus complex'.

In Meltzer's view all these investigations undermined Freud's existing theoretical preconceptions or speculations; of 'three Freuds' that he identifies (the obsessive theoretician, the politician guarding the 'party line', and the artist-clinician) it was the latter that moved inexorably towards working with the 'structural model' that corresponded to the whole-personalities that confronted him in real life, and to the realities of 'identification with an object in pain'; 'Freud was going to have to discard this energetics theory and the idea of un-pleasure, and really come to grips with a more purely psychological theory, in which 'pain' really was what it meant'. Meltzer believes that although Freud did not, in his theory of mind, ever fully confirm the shift away from the libido model (it shows more in his descriptive language that in his theorisation), yet the move from energetics to meaning and its organization marks the 'direction in which psychoanalysis has been directing its attention and development ever since'. And Freud, despite the pessimism of his last years, nonetheless exemplified the fact that 'there is no complete analysis: that any analysis is, at its best, a preparation for a continuation of self-scrutiny and development, and it is not meant to protect people from having conflicts in life, but only to equip them to meet these. Analysis is the beginning, and not the end, of a process.' And so it is with the analytic movement.

Meg Harris Williams
(editor)

Introduction to the series The Kleinian Development

I f we take the beginning of Anna O's treatment with Breuer as the start of the Psychoanalytical Era, 1980 would be its centenary.[1] There can be little doubt of the influence that this science has had upon Western thought and culture, both acknowledged and denied. It is certainly the premier method of clinical research into the deeper sources of personality development and functioning. It nourishes with its methodology and its discoveries a host of related disciplines. But it is not a unified discipline itself. It has developed in many different directions, in method, phenomenology, theory. The difficulty in describing the ineffable events of the consulting-room has widened the manifest gap between various lines of development, in a way that probably generates political groupings, where genuine disagreements, as against differing points of view, may very well be minimal. It is no tribute to the efficacy of psychoanalytical therapy, and its slight variant the training analysis, that analysts eagerly attach themselves to these political groupings and play

1 The *Kleinian Development* lectures were first published in 1978.

out in their societies dramas hardly distinguishable from the internal affairs of emergent nations. This volume is certainly not intended to enhance these polarizations. On the contrary, it seems reasonable to hope that a clarification of the particular line of development in psychoanalytical method and theory associated with the name of Melanie Klein might diminish the tensions, enabling people either to take an intelligent interest or an equally intelligent disinterest in this particular strand of scientific history. In order to do this it is necessary to review the development of Freud's work so as to identify the jumping-off place of Mrs Klein's thinking, and then to do the same with Bion *vis à vis* Freud and Klein.

This all sounds, of course, like an undertaking in scholarship but these three sets of lectures will be found to be most unscholarly. Although they are bound tightly to the literature of these three workers (only in one instance do I introduce any clinical experience of my own) , the approach is far too personal to pass academic muster. To explain this it is necessary to trace a little the history of the undertaking of these lectures. In the hope of following Milton's dictum of 'teaching others . . . himself may learn', yet being an unwilling student of the literature, I engaged myself in various commitments to force an indolent spirit. Six years of work and teaching to develop a new curriculum at the Institute of Psychoanalysis (subsequently abandoned because the students were dissatisfied with so historical and rigid a procedure) were followed by six years of teaching at the Tavistock Clinic, primarily to various classes in the training of child psychotherapists. These lectures therefore are the outcome of some twelve years of study and teaching aimed, in the secret egocentricity, at answering the questions in my own mind concerning the problems of continuity and discontinuity in my own development as a psychoanalyst.

From the age of sixteen, when I first read Freud under the influence of my elder sister's friend Nathaniel Apter, to the age of 22 when Loretta Bender (strangely) introduced me to the work of Melanie Klein, and on to the age of 40, when Bion 's personality and thought began to impinge upon me, my development has been dominated by transference to, and identification with, these three extraordinary people. But two events, Mrs Klein's death and Bion's subsequent departure for California, both of which served to disrupt a phantasy of family happiness amongst the followers of Mrs Klein, also served to make me aware that these three figures were not in a happy relation to one another in my mind and somehow also in my work.

I do not, of course, mean that I was concerned in any way with the history of their personal or professional relations, Freud to Klein or Klein to Bion. This was purely personal and internal to me, related to my own analysis obviously, my oedipal conflicts at various levels, etc., etc. But the infantile levels are not the central point for giving lectures although they may be for analysing dreams. The study and lecturing (and now the publication) were intended to discover and define the continuity or discontinuity in my psychoanalytical development in terms of success or failure to develop a combined psychoanalytical object 'under whose aegis' I might hope to work creatively and courageously some day.

Consequently the three sets of lectures that follow are a very personal integration of the work of these three people. My Freud, my Klein, my Bion may not correspond precisely with anyone else's. I would be distressed if they were not at least congruent with these figures in quite a few of my colleagues' minds. This somewhat tedious protest is not, however, without its point: namely to stress the absence of authority in what follows – neither my authority nor theirs; for not only are the lectures personal and therefore idiosyncratic, but they are also critical: a critique, non-reverential. This means also that they cannot stand alone but are meaningless except as an adjunct to serious study, a vademecum. For those who think they know the works of Freud, Klein and Bion well, the lectures should, if they succeed in their intention, come as a surprise that drives them back to the texts. For the beginning student they should serve as companion and guide. They are meant to assist in the organization of reading seminars and to help people in finding their way back to the literature for reference in writing papers. Above all they are meant to give one possible longitudinal view of this one line of development in psychoanalysis in a way that rectifies the conceptual confusions wrought by the overlapping of linguistic usage.

The overall burden of my song is that an unfolding can be seen in the work of these three masters when the language has been rectified, an unfolding of method, leading to discovery of new realms of phenomena, generating in turn new models of the mind, which then modify method, etc. The explicit (or implicit in the case of Mrs Klein), models of the mind I have called neuro-physiological, mythological (or theological) and philosophical. That they are not mutually exclusive but relate as root, trunk and branch to what flowers and fruits in the consulting room is my theme, my contention, probably my faith.

Introduction to Part 1: Freud's Clinical Development

These lectures were delivered in 1972 and 1973 to the students and guests of the Child Psychotherapy Course at the Tavistock Clinic, London. The students were largely in the first pre-clinical year of the course, so that the lectures served as background for acquaintance with Freud's work from reading seminars in this and in the following year. The aim of the lectures was to prepare the students for systematic study of the work of Melanie Klein by giving a firm foundation in Freud's writing on method, data and clinical formulation, somewhat at the expense of any systematic concern with his theory of the mind. Its emphasis was therefore heavily weighted on the clinical papers and on those aspects of his thought which can be seen to have had a development in Mrs Klein's work, It was also the intention to lecture in a critical way, searching out the order, meaning and significance of Freud's work rather than in any way to summarize it.

For this reason it is essential to the understanding of these lectures that the reader, like the student, should at least have refreshed his knowledge of the papers and books discussed, particularly the following (required) reading:

CHAPTER

I   *Studies on Hysteria. SE* II, 1–18, 21–47.

2   *Studies on Hysteria. SE* II, 135–182.
Further remarks on the neuropsychoses of defence, *SE* III, 159–187.
A specimen dream. *The Interpretation of Dreams, SE* IV, 106–121.

CHAPTER ONE

Why history?

The recommendation that people who are interested in learning to practise psychoanalytic therapy should apply themselves diligently to the study of Freud seems at first glance to scent of the cult of the personality, to ring of the gospel, and to suggest that nothing else is worthy of study. While it is certain that the recommendation has been used in all these ways, to the detriment of students and psychoanalysis alike, there is another rationale for the advice. There is a cogent justification which has to do with the essential nature of science: namely that it is truly rational in its history. This is formed around a thread of logical necessity. To borrow an image from Freud's early writing, in the history of psychoanalysis revelations or discoveries – whichever they be – adhere to a chain of logically necessary propositions as garlands of flowers wind about a wire.

It may be objected that this does not justify its discoveries being taught as the personal history of a particular worker, even if he can reasonably be called 'the father of psychoanalysis', or the greatest figure in its development, or the foremost authority, etc. It will be said, as it has been said, that Lavoisier was the father of chemistry, but we do not teach chemistry by starting with Lavoisier's life, not even his laboratory life, to say nothing of his intimate personal life. It is true that chemistry's history is not the history of people; its logical necessity lies in the relation of particles to one another under varying conditions. However, when you look at the curriculum for the training of chemistry scientists you will find that it adheres absolutely, of necessity, to a sequence which corresponds to the historical development of the science.

Furthermore, it may be objected that not even artists, who are positively addicted to history, study the intimate lives of their great forbears; only their works and methods. In short, only scholars and busybodies nose about in the personal biographies of great men. Perhaps. My concern here is not to give a scholarly exposition, nor is it to be a busybody; it is not with Freud's personal, intimate life, but with his works. I hope in fourteen chapters to construct an, not the, historical Freud: Freud the monument of literature, not really Freud the man; and above all, the Freud of this particular writer's – D. M.'s – imagination. This, of course, immediately presents itself as the most futile purpose of all, since D. M. never knew Freud. Would it not be better for him to present his personal Melanie Klein, or himself? Well, the latter would not do because no case could be made out for his being a key figure in psychoanalytic history. 'Why not Melanie Klein then? Well, for a perfectly good reason: relative lack of documentation. Consider, for instance, what you would do if you wanted to write the history of 13th century manorial life; you would not necessarily determine which was the biggest, most powerful, most successful, most beautiful or most anything-else manor, to study its manorial rolls. You would first determine which manorial rolls were the most completely preserved and select your manor accordingly. If this turned out to be the biggest, richest, etc., it would be only slightly wide of coincidental. Similarly, the documentation of Freud's scientific development is certainly not a function of his having been in any way superlative, but of his having been a compulsive writer. You must consider: 23 volumes of some 400 pages each; say about 9000 pages in 40-odd years. That comes to a book of over two hundred pages every year; twenty papers of ten pages each! In addition, by his hand, we have the letters to Fliess, the *Project for a Scientific Psychology*, letters to Abraham, and probably many more unpublished papers, case reports, etc., all guarded in the archives by the jealous dragon called Kurt Eissler. No, the most cogent reason for studying Freud is that he has left us a documentation of his thought and experience that is unparalleled.

Can we not, then, just forget that we are studying a man's life and works and concentrate on the material, the data, the method, the ideas? Suppose it were Newton; we would not, in studying the evolution of his work in mathematics, optics, etc., concern ourselves with his rather mad theological ramblings any more than we would with his sexual life. Indeed, we could ignore that aspect of Newton because his writings in theology are quite separate from his works in mathematics and physics. With Freud, however, as with the 13th century manorial rolls, fact and fancy, truth and distortion, new experiences and preconception, revelation and vituperation are all mixed together. We cannot say that we will study volumes III, V and VIII but not bother with IV, VI and VII. Nonetheless, a certain mode of concentration of effort is possible and is rewarding; namely, to stick very closely to the works that are clear in their clinical reference. And this is what we shall study: the case histories, dream interpretation, technical papers; and draw on the major theoretical works only for the light they throw on the more clinical ones. There is another sorting device we can also use, though more cautiously. We can use the 1895 *Project* as a template for identifying preconceptions in Freud's thinking about his data.

This is a somewhat delicate process which requires some explanation and an historic setting to make it understandable. Looking back through the agency of the 'Autobiography', Jones's biography, the Fliess letters, the *Project* and others, one is surely struck by the incongruity of the young Freud *vis à vis* the great Freud, the revolutionary. Of course, we tend to be blasé about the psychoanalytical revolution today, in consequence of which the embattled Freud of the 1890s tends to be as unreal to us as the barricades of 1848. But he was a revolutionary of the methodical-constructive rather than the rebellious-destructive sort and his early scientific career gives no hint of the future. He seems to have been one of the innumerable young men whom medical science, in its historical heyday, gathered to it for many reasons – of adventure, glamour, status, economic possibilities. For a young Jew these attractions were all potentiated. And how wide were his interests: the cocaine experiment, histology, neuropathology, clinical neurology, and only latterly psychiatry. Many letters suggest the impatience of the parvenu, the opportunist, seeking alliances with promising contemporaries, currying favour with the great tyrants who ruled the laboratories and wards like oriental potentates, offering his services as translator, taking the burden of routine lectures. Of course it is tempting to weave an Ariadne-like thread from the staining of motor neurones through the paralyses of children to the motor manifestations of hysteria: and in a way the *Project* offers itself as such a 'web': but it is not really true. If it were, a very different concept of growth and development of the mind would be required from that which psychoanalysis offers – one which would see the mind like a blossom unfolding in all its beauty and perfection, given a suitable environment. Gone would be the ideas of conflict and decision; realization of error, remorse, reparation.

The greatness of Freud did not unfold like a blossom and its environment was far from congenial. The clinical method of description and isolation of syndromes and the investigation of predisposing, specific and contributory aetiological factors was establishing a nosology which was lifting medicine out of a welter of confusion, quackery and noxious meddling. Great names were beginning to take their place in history through therapeutic and prophylactic achievements, particularly in bacteriology.

In this golden tradition, not more than a century old, psychiatry was taking shape through classification, generally now associated with the name of Kraepelin. This carried the implication that in due course, aetiologies would be discovered, cures and preventions would be evolved. It was an optimistic era in every way! The great mental hospitals were the laboratories of the descriptive science, and access to them was as prized then as access to a cyclotron or a huge computer is now by physicists. It seemed that nothing could be done without access to these great pools of clinical material. One must also remember what a bourgeois world it was and the Jewish and commercial tradition that lay behind Freud. The aim was clearly to make a name for oneself as expert and authority in a small segment of the whole and gradually to expand one's kudos, territory and hegemony. Today, over a century since his birth, is the climate so different for the medical student and young scientist, despite the apparent advance of social consciousness and responsibility?

Freud was a child of his time, a 'normal' and 'well-adjusted' person (if we must use these banal descriptive and normative concepts) and he tried to make his mark in the bourgeois world: with cocaine, neuro-pathology, paralyses of children, aphasia and finally hysteria. The dependent aspects of his character demanded support and encouragement. The list which starts with Meynert and Breuer and grows so tenuous with Fliess does not really stop for another decade until the defection of Jung, when Freud is about 55 years old. The methodology and social order were set about him in solid phalanx against the development of the psychoanalytical method. Nor was there yet really a 'mind' to be studied. It would be erroneous today to think of depth psychology as a well-established field of scientific enquiry, with psychoanalysis as its premier method. Perhaps even more today than at the time of Freud's death, the concept of 'the mind is the brain' holds the field against that of 'mind as phenomenon'. In Freud's youth the 'phenomenon' was still the realm of theologians, metaphysicians and cosmologists. The practical bourgeois world had turned its back and closed its laboratory doors to such thinking. How ironic, in this context, to think that the most appreciative review that the *Studies on Hysteria* received was from a professor of the history of literature, entitled 'Surgery of the soul'. One wonders if this did not cause a shudder of anxiety rather than a tingle of pleasure in Freud.

Nor is it surprising that an historian should be the prophet, for psychoanalysis teaches us that the acknowledgement of the past as the foundation of the present is the only means of making the concept of 'future' obedient to reason. Lacking this obedience to continuity, the idea of 'future' loses its meaning and simply becomes equated with 'wish' or 'intention'. In the same way every student of psychoanalysis must traverse in his ontogeny the history of this peculiar scientific species of ours. Each of us has been brought up in a milieu from whose values, methods and aspirations we need, gradually, to free ourselves in order to learn, utilise and make discoveries by — the psychoanalytical method. In a sense we also need to abandon, in Freud's words, 'the expectation of lasting fame, the certainty of wealth and complete independence': as he did when the 'seduction theory', the 'specific aetiology' of hysteria crumbled at the revelation that infantile sexual phantasies had been confused with memories by both patients and investigator.

Here too, in the realm of social and personal attitudes toward sexuality, we must avoid smugness. A century has produced a great swing of the pendulum, not a little of which has been rightly attributed to the impact of Freud's work on western culture. But the pendulum has swung from the hypocrisy of the Victorian double standard to the hypocrisy of decadence. The milieu which favoured the formation of symptoms in the realm of sexual conflict now favours the hardening of perversion into character. As Freud had to face the suspicion of being an 'a moralist', today's believer in psychic reality will need to face, internally and externally, the even more sanctimonious charge of 'moralist'. No use for us to smile indulgently at the trepidation with which he put forward to his colleagues the need to investigate the sexual life of the psychoneurotic. The icy epithet of 'fairy-tale' he faced is unchanged today, only directed against the investigation of the immediate reality of the mind rather than the past reality of traumatic experiences.

There can be no doubt that Freud paid heavily for his arrogance in placing his evidence first before public values. He could have written as freely as he wished about sexuality had he, like Krafft-Ebing and others, dealt with the pathological behaviour as symptoms of underlying disease rather than as aetiological factors in themselves; had he confined himself to the perverse activities of adults and the masturbation of children. But by assaulting the mores with an insistence on the significance of *lack* of satisfaction, of sexual needs in adults and the reality of sexual *capacity* in childhood, he opposed the 'scientific' and 'progressive' spirit of the age. The Fliess letters tell the story: from the elation which culminated in the *Project* (1895), soon followed by the catastrophe of the collapse of the 'seduction' theory (1897), to the self-analysis, whose brain child was *The Interpretation of Dreams*; and the resolution of the ambivalent relation to Fliess, whose fruit is the 'Letters' itself. The mounting clinical evidence in favour

of the 'seduction' theory had begun to invade Freud's own relationships past and present, as it began to seem statistically likely
that all parents committed incestuous assaults on their children.
The incongruity – and the anxiety coming closer to home, along
with the upheaval of his father's death – must have been powerful
factors in the inception of the systematic self-analysis. But while
the anxiety drove Freud, in his step toward greatness, to apply the
method to himself, it could only be expected, as a source of social
anxiety, to generate hostility. After the 'seduction' theory, which
could be coldly rejected as a 'fairy tale', came the great steps
toward recognition of the universality of the unconscious: the
Traumdeutung (1900), *Psychopathology of Everyday Life* (1901),
Wit and its Relation to the Unconscious (1905), and *Three Essays
on Sexuality* (1905). What a manifesto! And how he paid for it
with isolation, abuse, contempt, the threat of poverty.

But, of course, every crank and crackpot pays this price for
insisting on the validity of his intuitions, any of which may in fact
turn out to be correct. Freud, like other creative geniuses, paid the
price of devotion to a method, the findings of which inevitably
turned out to be wrong! For instance, all that Freud says about
hysteria can now be considered 'wrong' because there is no such
thing as 'hysteria' in the sense in which it was discussed by
Charcot in Paris, Bernheim in Zurich or Breuer in Vienna, at
the turn of the century. You may recall that the paucity of interest in Freud's work among his Viennese colleagues was partly an
expression of apathy about hysteria itself. They could not take
it seriously as a 'disease' but considered it to be some elaborate
form of malingering, until the experiments with hypnosis repro-
duced its clinical phenomenology: or rather, until it was proven
that hypnosis was not an elaborate form of suggestion – which
it is! Similarly, it might be cogently argued that the whole idea
of psychopathology is 'wrong' and that we should leave it out of
the curriculum as the theory of 'humours' is left out of a modern
course in pathophysiology. Has not psychoanalysis abandoned
the concepts of 'disease' and 'cure' and become the field of 'depth
psychology' that it is so often called? So here again, the swing of
the pendulum presents today's student with the same problems
within his culture that Freud faced, only upside down, you might
say. His evidence could be thrown out of court by the establishment

because it was gained from study of 'diseased' minds and could therefore bear no relation to 'normality'. Today the evidence of psychoanalysis regarding psychic reality, the primacy of internal experience over external, the relation of 'health' and the values connected with the 'good' are similarly ignored on the grounds that there is no good; all is relative, semantic, unmeasurable; therefore unreal. Freud grasped slowly (and we must allow for the possibility that we will grasp even more slowly) that the study of psychopathology was the entrée to the mind, if only a method could be found which passed beyond mere external description. Perhaps this realisation was more available to a neurologist than it would have been to a surgeon, physician or pathologist, for whom the most imposing situations were those analogous to an invasion of a closed system by alien chemicals, objects, bacteria, protozoa, etc. Embryology of the individual appeared to be complete long before birth, except for increasing size and maturation of the sexual organs. Even neuro-embryology seemed to reach completion shortly after birth. But in the methods of examination and the near-mathematical localizing diagnosis of the neurologist alone amongst clinical fields, the interruption of normal functioning took pride of place over the questions of abnormal function and specific aetiology. Furthermore, studies in neuropathology of childhood showed how different could be the clinical phenomena of a lesion, depending on the age of the patient: whether it was interfering with the development of new functions, or destroying functions already established and thus allowing more primitive ones to reappear.

These principles of neurological localization and their reference to a developmental process came gradually to impose themselves on Freud and to wrest from his mind the neurophysiological preconceptions of the *Project*. In this departure from the concrete, and in his extraordinarily open-minded and non-moralistic approach to sexuality, he broke with the community and became an outcast, propounding a theory of the mind as a developmental phenomenon whose units were thoughts, not neuron, whose energies were impulses with aims seeking objects, whose dislocations produced anxieties, whose traumas could not be apprehended descriptively but only in relation to the momentary state of mind.

Again we must turn to the present community to recognize that this developmental conception of psychopathology is as intensely resisted now as it was then; again the pendulum has swung. As with the false dichotomy of the mind–body problem, so are we confronted with the false dichotomy of the nature–nurture problem. It is difficult to avoid being embroiled in it, in the treacle of sanctimony, placing the blame (as if psychoanalysis had anything to do with placing blame) on the parents or on the child, on the community, the times, fate, sunspots, or God! With the realisation in 1897 of the falsity of the 'seduction' theory of hysteria, Freud leapt forward to the realization of developmental conflict, resistance and the transference. The conflicts – and resistances – are no less today and no less in us than in the Viennese of 70 years ago. Only the form of the resistance is altered.

An instructive way of recognising how Freud was bound by the modes of thought of his milieu and had to struggle to free himself lies in a study of the imagery, models and analogies that he employs in his writing. I will give a series of these chronologically, to demonstrate the trend.

1. *Studies on Hysteria* – 1893–95
'The point at which a symptom' (of hysteria) 'has already broken through once forms a weak spot at which it will break through again the next time. A psychical group that has once been split off plays the part of a 'provoking' crystal from which a crystallisation which would otherwise not have occurred will start with the greatest facility.' (*SE* 11, p. 264)

2. *The Neuropsychoses of Defence* –1894
'In mental functions something is to be distinguished – a quota of affect or sum of excitation – which possesses all the characteristics of a quantity (though we have no means of measuring it), which is capable of increase, diminution, displacement and discharge, and which is spread over the memory – traces of ideas somewhat as an electric charge is spread over the surface of a body.' (*SE* III, p. 60)

3. *The Aetiology of Hysteria* – 1896
'In hysteria too there exists a similar possibility of penetrating from the symptoms to a knowledge of their causes. But in order to explain the relationship between

the method which we have to employ for this purpose and the older method of anamnestic inquiry, I should like to bring before you an analogy taken from an advance that has in fact been made in another field of work.

'Imagine that an explorer arrives at a little-known region where his interest is aroused by an expanse of ruins, with remains of walls, fragments of columns, and tablets with half-effaced and unreadable inscriptions. He may content himself with inspecting what lies exposed to view, with questioning the inhabitants – perhaps semi-barbaric people – who live in the vicinity, about what tradition tells them of the history and meaning of these archaeological remains, and with noting down what they tell him – and he may then proceed on his journey. But he may act differently. He may have brought picks, shovels and spades with him, and he may set the inhabitants to work with these implements. Together with them he may start upon the ruins, clear away the rubbish, and, beginning from the visible remains, uncover what is buried. If his work is crowned with success, the discoveries are self-explanatory ...' (*SE* III, p. 192)

– the optimist!

These are three examples from the pre-self-analysis period, of analogies regarding symptom formation, psychic energy and methodology. Compare:

4. *Fragment of an analysis of a case of hysteria* (1905; written in 1901):

(a) 'Contrary thoughts are always closely connected with each other and are often paired off in such a way that the one thought is *excessively intensely conscious while its counterpart is repressed and unconscious.* This relation between the two thoughts is an effect of the process of repression. For repression is often achieved by means of an excessive reinforcement of the thought contrary to the one which is to be repressed. This process I call *reactive* reinforcement, and the thought which assets itself with excessive intensity in consciousness and (in the same way as a prejudice) cannot be removed I call a *reactive thought.* The two thoughts then act toward each other much like the two needles of an astatic galvanometer. The reactive thought keeps the objectionable one under repression by means of a certain surplus of intensity; but for that reason it itself is "damped" and proof against conscious efforts of thought.' (*SE* VII, p. 55)

(b) 'The *motive force* which the dream required had to be provided by a wish; it was the business of the worry to get hold of a wish to act as the motive force of a dream.

'The position may be explained by an analogy. A daytime thought may very well play the part of an entrepreneur for a dream; but the entrepreneur, who, as people say, has the idea and the initiative to carry it out, can do nothing without capital; he needs a *capitalist* who can afford the outlay, and the *capitalist* who provides the psychical outlay for the dream is invariably and indisputably, whatever may be the thoughts of the previous day, a wish from the unconscious.' (p. 87)

(c) 'What are transferences? They are new editions or fac-similes of the impulses and phantasies which are aroused and made conscious during the progress of the analysis; but they have this peculiarity, which is characteristic of their species, that they replace some earlier person by the person of the physician. To put it another way: a whole series of psycho-logical experiences are reviewed, not as belonging to the past, but as applying to the person of the physician at the present moment. Some of these transferences have a content which differ from that of their model in no respect whatever except for substitution. These then – to keep to the same metaphor – are merely new impressions or reprints. Others are more ingeniously constructed; their content has been subjected to a moderating influence –*to sublimation*, as I call it – and they may even become conscious, by cleverly taking advantage of some real peculiarity in the physician's person or circum-stances and attaching them selves to that. These, then, will no longer be new editions, but revised editions.' (p. 116)

Well, we need go no further. The change is clear, I am sure. The literal and mechanical quality of the earlier models has given way to imaginative, near poetic, and vital images and models in the later writing. For instance, examine the rather dramatic 'archaeological' model from the *Studies*. What Freud is describing is the reconstruction of the environment of the ancient culture, its houses, temples, markets, tools, organization of services, technology. These are 'self-explanatory'. But the life of the people is not, and can only be found in the written record. You may remember that Sir Arthur Evans had recently – 1898 or so – excavated Knossos and Mycaenae, uncovering great treasure, and Linear B. But no Napoleon presented him with a Rosetta Stone with which to translate this script. It had to wait sixty years until the techniques of cryptography and etymology could be brought together in a wonderfully creative way by Michael Ventris (see John Chadwick, *The Decipherment of Linear B*, 1958) for the life of the people to be revealed. Freud seems to have had the idea that dreams were the Rosetta Stone of the unconscious and he their translator. We can see more clearly how he underestimated the difficulty. Perhaps they are the Linear B of the unconscious!

In the first chapter I am discussing the period of Freud's work as a psychotherapist, which is fundamentally prior to the development of the basic psychoanalytical method. You will recall that Freud was a neurologist and research worker in clinical neurology by training and experience: take for example the work on aphasia and the paralyses of children, and neuroanatomy, particularly the central pathways which he was investigating by special silver staining techniques. He did not easily become a psychologist, and it was not until 1910 that he gave himself that name. His interest in the work of Charcot in Paris, Liebault in Nancy and Bernheim in Zurich was not primarily directed toward an understanding of the mind, but of the brain. The phenomenology of divided consciousness, fugue states, hypnosis, suggestion and dreams attracted his interest not as vicissitudes of people's emotional and intellectual experiences of life, but as evidences of the complex working of the brain and of its malfunction. The possibility of brain damage, inherited tendencies, degenerative disease (and of course the universal suspicion of central nervous system syphilis) hung constantly in the periphery of his mind. His initial approach to what was to become his life's work, his collaboration with Breuer and the publication of the *Studies on Hysteria* (1895), was a purely medical one, which sought the relief of symptoms. In a sense it stood in the same relation to his great love, neurophysiology, as had the experiment with cocaine. It was a bid for status and it almost wrecked him, as we shall see. When we study in some detail the famous dream of Irma's injection from the *Traumdeutung*, it will become clearer how the ambition-which-impairs-judgment haunted Freud, and how he struggled against it by constructing a method by which he could impose some basic discipline on himself. He was by this time a young man no longer – married, with children – aged nearly forty years. He had tried many ways of advancing himself in the Austrian medical establishment by working in the university hospital, doing research, translating the work of Charcot, lecturing. But of course the opportunities were relatively poor for a Jew. The record sounds fairly opportunistic, and there can be little doubt that he was a highly ambitious man who felt his prime slipping away from him with very little to show for it. The mishaps with cocaine weighed heavily on him and failure to receive recognition for pioneering its legitimate use embittered him.

Accordingly, Freud's sections of the *Studies* have a tone that contrasts sharply with the humble one of Breuer who was awed by the phenomena, somewhat enamoured of his intelligent patient, Anna O., and basically unwilling to reveal to the world a relationship which had ended in the shock of Anna's erotic attachment to him and in near tragedy owing to his wife's intense jealousy over the matter. It is clear in the joint 'Preliminary communication' (1893) that Breuer was a fairly unwilling participant in the publication, and that an undercurrent of disagreement swamped the relationship. Freud of course was relatively young, unestablished, and in that sense riding on Breuer's high reputation, probably more dependent on the older man than he realised. As the relationship cooled after the publication of the *Studies* it seems to have been replaced by the intimacy with Fliess, but here Freud recognised his dependence, and in a sense his ambivalence and exploitation, insincerity and high-handedness toward the other man. In the *Studies* we meet a fairly unexceptional man in Freud and a rather impressive one in Breuer. Ten years later, in the 'Fragment' on Dora we will meet a great man. How did the change come about and what were the scientific experiences and accomplishments that accompanied or moved this transformation? Let us start by taking stock of Freud as he reveals himself in the *Studies* side by side with Breuer – and with his patients.

CHAPTER TWO

The spiral of method and data
(*Studies on Hysteria*)

In the first chapter I suggested that the fate of the creative scientist, as compared with the intuitive crank, is to be
'wrong' in all his conclusions. Freud knew this very well
and for this reason never hesitated to publish his current
ideas nor to abandon them for later approximations. If we
try to take the measure of the history of psychoanalysis from
the theoretical point of view, we would be in the maelstrom of
swirling ideas, models, imagery, from which we would only
escape by an arbitrary grasping at what Freud said – in the
Introductory Lectures for instance but not in 'The ego and
the id' – or, worse still, to establish our own reading of Freud
as *the* correct one: i.e. an orthodoxy.

But science (and art, for that matter) is not carried forward
by theories but by advances in method, in technique. Jokingly
one may say that the inventor of psychoanalysis was Anna O.
with her 'talking cure' and 'chimney sweeping', and I would
think that Freud was sincere when in the 1910 lectures at
Clark University he gave credit for the origin to Breuer.

Although this famous case is so badly presented, compared
with the flow and lucidity of Freud's writing, one is struck with
the immense time, interest, concern, ingenuity, patience – and

modesty — with which the clinical work and collection of data were carried out. This is perhaps the best evidence we can obtain in order to understand why Breuer stood so high in the younger Freud's esteem and to give him his rightful place in psychoanalytic history. Remember that the therapeutic methodology of the day was utterly different: sedation, warm baths, faradic current stimulation for the paralyses, massage for the contractures — anything but attention to the mind of the patient. One might say that the phenomenology of hysteria was dealt with as mental by the hypnotists, but only in the sense of 'trauma' impinging on a defective apparatus, not as experience affecting a sensitive person. Breuer's admiration for Anna O.'s character and intellect, his respect for her as a person and his therapeutic intent seem to have been leading his scientific curiosity and perhaps left him too vulnerable to the anxiety which her erotic transference aroused. But it was an attitude strongly in contrast to the contempt of his times for the 'neuropathic' and the 'degenerate'. By comparison with the older man, we tend to find the younger Freud of the Studies harder, more ambitious, his therapeutic drive more egocentric. Only the touching fragment of 'Katarina', the girl of the Alpine village, reveals the depth of warmth and tender concern which can later be seen in relation to 'Dora' or 'Little Hans'. Is it not interesting that the tenderness then was similarly accompanied by vulnerability, for Dora hurt Freud as Anna O. frightened Breuer? But while the latter was driven by the pain away from further investigation, the great man grasped the nettle and comprehended for the first time the crucial significance of the transference in the psychoanalytical method.

Let us return for a moment, then, to the 'joke' that Anna O. was the originator of the psychoanalytical method. Personally I take it quite seriously that the history of our science is one of collaborative investigation by patient and analyst and would not have the slightest hesitation in saying that the essence of the method is one in which the 'patient' is always the 'investigator' and that self-analysis is the key to the process. Clearly the greatest of the 'patients' would be the fellow whom Freud analysed in his self-analysis. Taken from this point of view, the whole of our literature may be read as self-revelation by its various authors. Does this perhaps give some clue to the great difficulty in analytic writing, the amount of anxiety it engenders, the courage it requires? Reading the case of Anna O. supplies ample evidence of the creativity of this young woman, and Breuer is surely telling the truth when he says that 'it took me completely by surprise, and not until symptoms had been got rid of in this way' (i.e. the 'talking cure') 'in a whole series of instances did I develop a therapeutic technique of it' (i.e. the 'cathartic method').

What was Anna O.'s method, then? First of all it consisted of states of 'autohypnosis' in which she 'talked out' all the hallucinatory and anxiety phantasy experience of the day. Then she evolved an anamnestic period in which she talked out the internal events of the corresponding day of the previous year (1880–81). Thirdly she set a time period of one year to the process, declaring that she would stop on the anniversary of her being moved into the country after her father's death. (When it happened ten years later that the illness of the young Mathilde H. self-terminated on the anniversary of the breaking of her engagement, Freud recognised the link to mourning processes and that the credit received for the cure by his hypnosis was spurious [p. 163]). Fourthly, Anna O. traced back in association current symptoms to their initial appearance. Fifthly, she found the link between symptoms and dreams, especially the moving dream of the snake. In the end she investigated the problem of the reality of 'the unconscious' and its relation to the splitting in herself with regard to the problem of the 'will', convincing Breuer, perhaps more than herself, that her pathological states of 'naughtiness' had been beyond her control, even if only in the sense that the 'will' to control their outward manifestation was lacking.

So impressive is Anna O.'s performance that today one would question the diagnosis of hysteria and tend to consider her illness one of neurotic depressive reaction connected with impeded mourning, the prognosis of which was probably good and self-terminating – for is not the mourning process a self analytical one of its very nature? In discussing the part played by nursing the dying in the aetiology of his cases, Freud suggests as much (p. 162). Recall that Anna O.'s illness, or at least the aspects of it treated by Breuer, ended in June 1882 and the *Studies* were published in 1895, two years after the 'Preliminary communication'. Compare this thirteen years of 'incubation' of the method with the next ten years, which saw the realisation of the great seminal works of psychoanalysis – the *Interpretation of Dreams*, *Psychopathology of Everyday Life*, *Wit and its Relation to the Unconscious*, 'Fragment of analysis of a case of hysteria', and *Three Essays on Sexuality*. Remember the crucial year 1897, the collapse of the 'traumatic' theory and the beginning of Freud's self-analysis. To follow the development set in train by Anna O. and Breuer, let us examine the evolution as revealed in the cases themselves: Emmy von N. (1889), Lucy R. (1892), Dora (1900). These of course are treatment and not publication dates.

Emmy von N.'s physician is a stranger to us and not a very likeable one, I fear. As Freud says, he was completely under the sway of Bernheim's method of suggestion and appears also not to have liked his patient very much. We may not find this surprising, as it is doubtful that she would be considered an hysteric today, but rather a severe obsessional character with marked paranoid trends, diffuse hypochondria, and somatic delusions as well as hysterical symptoms. The treatment consisted of two brief periods, seven and perhaps nine weeks long, separated by a year, with a brief follow-up visit one year later and a note three years later indicating a relapse. The tone of the description is unpleasantly assertive, shallow and arrogant, in keeping with the methods – and the data is rather boring. The method was as follows: warm and cool baths, massaging 'her body all over' each day and then hypnosis each evening, during which a description of her fears and symptoms was elicited along with their chronology – reported in reverse order, as with Anna O. The disappearance of these symptoms would then be ordered by the so-called 'suggestion'. Freud seems to have told her 'white lies', cautionary tales, played hypnotic and post-hypnotic tricks and finally tyrannised over her with an ultimatum (about drinking alkaline waters). Her attempts to induce him to listen more to her recollections found at best irritable compliance, in contrast with the friendly response of Breuer to Anna O.'s similar request. It is however very interesting to see, from a footnote, that Freud was systematically analysing his own dreams at this time, though not consciously for the purpose of self-analysis: rather as part of the work on the *Interpretation of Dreams*, studying the day-residue, false connections, compulsion to associate, etc. But Freud's own sad footnote of 1924 reminds us to save the 'smile of pity' for our own poor efforts.

In the brief treatment of Lucy R. (only nine weeks) we find a different man, using a different method. He has found himself an indifferent hypnotist and is now relying upon 'forcing' associations by pressure of his hand on the forehead. Obviously delighted to have been able to dispense with the hocus-pocus of the hypnotic situation, he is more able to think, speak and feel with his patient. Note, for instance, how in the discussion of the splitting of consciousness and forgetting, he refers his understanding of the process in his patient's mind to similar events in his own (p. 117). His intuition is alive and his approach, as when he suggests to Lucy that she is in love with her employer, is both bold and tender. The case is hardly a 'case, at all, but rather a transient hysterical symptom, accompanying a period of mild depression in an unmarried woman secretly in love, attached to the children and husband of her deceased mistress. But the patient's fundamental mental health also misled Freud into underestimating the inaccessibility of the repressed, for in his discussion of this case he almost begs the question of the unconsciousness of the 'traumatic' event. This is extremely important in relation to the development of the method, which was still excessively directed toward the resolution of symptoms and therefore bound to therapeutic success as the test of theoretical formulation. Neither Emmy von N., Lucy R. nor Katarina led Freud back to dreams nor to early childhood with the same creative relentlessness that was exerted on Breuer by Anna O. What Freud had said about the *Studies* is so true. The clinical material read like 'short stories', all about human relations, feelings, hopes, phantasies – and the discussions read like accounts of the physiology laboratory. The cleavage between the clinician and the theoretician in Freud is so apparent, for he had not yet begun to struggle against the hope, expressed in the *Project* of 1895, of reducing psychology to neurophysiological, quantifiable items, with Greek letters as a notation.

The 'first full length analysis', as Freud called it, also reads like a short story, but important advances in technique already had declared themselves in relation to Elizabeth von R. and new data was impinging on Freud's mind. Again the pressure technique was used in lieu of hypnosis generally and the 'excavation' of the material 'layer by layer' was meticulously pursued – by which he meant tracing the so-called 'causal chain' of memories (not association, notice) back to the original trauma, which was then to be fully 'abreacted'. Freud found this attractive, 'cheeky' and 'cock-sure' girl of 24 far less docile when confronted with secret longings for her deceased sister's husband, than had been the governess Lucy R. from Glasgow. But he faced this storm (which he calls 'resistance' for the first time) manfully, and 'consoled' the distressed young woman in two ways: that she was not responsible for her feelings, and that her illness was testimony to her good character. Amusing Victorian consolation, but it brings into focus an important aspect of this 'full length analysis': namely that Freud became deeply identified with the girl, one suspects, and went far beyond relieving her symptoms. He sought actively to bring about Elizabeth's marriage to her brother-in-law by way of a discussion with the mother, for which the patient probably never forgave him. He says ruefully about her not returning to see him in follow-up that 'it is characteristic of the personal relationship which arises in treatment of this kind': a harbinger of the concept of the 'transference', and an indication of the pain of the countertransference.

These phenomena we must link with Freud's evasiveness about the entire problem of infantile sexuality and incestuous desires, as evidenced in the distortion of the clinical material with both Katarina and Rosalie H., where he altered the references to sexual conflict from the father to an 'uncle'. By leading his patients in the enquiry, rather than following, as Breuer had done with Anna O., he could only find confirmation for his theories of retention, multiple trauma, symbolisation etc., while preventing the patient's tendency (mentioned in almost every case) to follow associations back into early childhood.

No, one must recognise that Anna O. herself is the heroine of the *Studies,* and Freud's future greatness only peeps through in his discussion of the psychotherapeutic method, where we can see that the experiences were impinging on him and making him re-think his preconceptions. These elements stand out: first, the growing sensitivity to the mental pain in the patient which manifests itself as resistance to the investigations when the crucial memories were approached; secondly, the resistance due to the transference, for it is here that the concept is erected for the first time into an essential component of the method.

When we turn to the case of Dora, five years after the publication of the *Studies,* we are astonished at the change in the man and can hardly find evidence in the published writings of the intervening period to trace the metamorphosis in method and in mastery. The Fliess letters tell us only the drama of the evolution of the theoretician, not of the clinician, in whom we are more interested. We can see from the evidence cited in the various papers of 1894–97 that the methods we have already discussed were leading him to the discovery of the important role of sexuality – abstinence, lack of satisfaction, infidelity, masturbation and perversion – in the adult lives of his patients and, with increasing frequency, the recollection of passive traumatic sexual experiences in childhood at the hands of adults, followed by active experiences with other children in the case of the obsessional patients. By 1897 the 'seduction' theory had collapsed, and the self-analysis had begun wherein Freud was to discover the Oedipus complex and the universality of infantile sexuality. But of course, the clinical method and data are not available to us, except for a peep under the tent in the papers on forgetfulness, screen memories, and in the books of this period – the *Traumdeutung, Wit,* and *Everyday Life.*

In the next chapter we will turn to the great Freud in his clinical work with Dora and see again how the new methods were bringing new data which enriched the psychopathology of hysteria. To review briefly: in this second chapter I have traced the evolution of the method by its various contributors – Anna O., Breuer and Freud – in a way which was intended to show how the changing data thrown into relief constitutes the real substance of the concepts of psychopathology. The theories I have merely alluded to, as they are less important than the phenomenology, since we are dealing mainly with Freud's views on psychopathology and not with the evolution of the psychoanalytical theory of the mind.

CHAPTER THREE

The crystallisation of the method dream analysis (Dora)

The great Freud and the psychoanalytical revolution really begin at the inception of the self-analysis in 1897, after the collapse of the 'seduction' theory of hysteria, the 'specific aetiology'. We may safely assume that the writing of the *Traumdeutung* (1900), *Wit*, and *Everyday Life*, belong to the epoch of the 'cathartic method' in which Freud's interest in the working of the mind was beginning to separate itself from the neurophysiologist's interest in the brain. He was working with new ideas: splitting of consciousness, retention of affects, mental pain due to unacceptable ideas, psychic trauma, etc., applied essentially to old data available to psychiatrists. In his isolation, he still hoped for a fair hearing and scientific interest in his findings. Even in the introduction to 'Dora', where he both pleads for a hearing and defends himself against foreseen criticism, he is of the opinion that the data is available to any psychiatrist who will take the trouble to collect it. It seems naive and amusing for Freud to suggest that anyone who follows the directions in the recipe book, the *Traumdeutung*, can analyse dreams. And we know in fact that as late as 1910 he said that anyone who would analyse his own dreams could practise the new science.

We must conclude that the clinical work revealed in the case of 'Dora', done in 1900, shows a development of technical virtuosity in Freud which he did not recognise himself. How it should have arisen in the five short years since the publication of the *Studies*, or rather in the three short years since the collapse of the 'seduction' theory (for this is when the method changed), we can hardly imagine. We must simply take as given, that Freud's genius was in full spate for the first time and the outpouring between 1900 and 1905 is incredible. More incredible still is the fact that, as you will see later on, this spate was repeated in the period 1920–26, from 'Beyond the pleasure principle' to 'Inhibition, symptom and anxiety'. An early flowering, age circa 45 – and a late flowering, age circa 65.

But only with the writing of 'Dora', which he viewed mainly as a 'supplement' (p. 114) to the *Traumdeutung* rather than as a continuation of the *Studies*, does the truth seem to come through to Freud, that he has invented a way of penetrating the depths of the mind through its pathology and that its data cannot be available except to those who can – and do – faithfully follow the method. You will recall that he writes in the Postscript: 'I have in this paper left entirely out of account the technique, which does not at all follow as a matter of course, but by whose means alone the pure metal of valuable unconscious thoughts can be extracted from the raw material of the patient's associations. This brings with it the disadvantage of the reader being given no opportunity of testing the correctness of my procedure.' Not until the technical papers of the 1910–14 period did he describe the technique, but from 'Dora' we can derive it. Because we keep in mind that 'Dora' is a landmark in the development of the psychoanalytical method since in it Freud recognised the methodological importance of the transference for the first time, we will look for evidence particularly of transference interpretations – but in vain. Only in the postscript, where Freud acknowledges that his failure to analyse the transference led to the premature interruption of the treatment after three months, will we find an example of what he wished he had said (p. 118) to elicit evidence of the transference.

So from the point of view of the methodological importance of the transference, 'Dora' is a negative landmark. But in other respects we can see the technical advances in action. The clinical data of the marvellously written study shows, as the introduction proclaims, that Freud had abandoned the 'pressure' method of 'forcing' associations for a new one of free association (so-called) or, really, that he had ceased to lead and was now content to follow the patient. In consequence the inevitable references to early childhood *development*, and not merely traumatic incidents, stand forth. The humanity with which Freud traces Dora's development is very different from the romanticism with which he investigated the love-life of Lucy R. or Elizabeth von R. The coolness and suspension of moral judgment with which he traces her normal and perverse sexual interests is very changed from the icy detachment with which he guarded himself from recognizing his identification with Elizabeth, for instance. We can believe, in reading this case, that the *Three Essays on Sexuality*, derived from his clinical experience in the treatment of neuroses and that it cannot be taken as preconception which he imposed upon the material. See the way in which he has elicited the information from the eighteen-year-old Dora of her knowledge about fellatio, linking it to her childhood habit of thumb-sucking and ear-pulling; how he assumes that the symptoms of pressure sensation on her thorax after the kiss, at age fourteen by Herr K. was a displacement of the sensation of pressure from Herr K.'s erect penis; how he joins her childhood symptoms of aphonia to her being a poor eater; how the heterosexual and homosexual aspects of her relation to the K's is connected with the easy shift from nipple to penis as object of oral cravings in childhood.

In all of these evidences of facility of thought and virtuosity of linking we see unmistakeable evidence of a different man from the psychotherapist of the *Studies*. Note also that when Freud mentions the care with which he sought evidence of Dora's existing knowledge of sexuality, he boldly declares that he did so, not to avoid the charge of corrupting an innocent girl but to avoid contaminating the reliability of his data. Really, one must be a little aghast at the courage of this lonely man at the turn of the century. The method had seized him and he was pressing on with the excitement – nay, recklessness – which only the thrill of the pursuit of knowledge can explain. The traits of ambition and the urgency of the parvenu are gone. And with them is banished the therapeutic test of theoretical validity – as for instance when he hesitates to claim a success in eliminating Dora's nervous cough. How bold indeed to publish such a 'fragment' of unsuccessful treatment altogether. Clearly the internal validity of the data about the human being in question has become the testing ground. Correspondingly, we see that Freud's thinking has abandoned final causes and has embraced 'overdetermination' as the principle for the comprehension of the symptoms. Even a formula such as the one that 'neurosis is the negative of perversions, is not put forward in a mechanistic sense but rather with a view to considering the neurosis as the sexual life *per se* of the neurotic person. But we will return to this in a little while when we come to take stock of the change in the nature of the whole concept of psychopathology which inheres in the psychoanalytical revolution that took place in those few years. Before turning to that stock-taking, we must pay some attention to the two dreams and the method of dream analysis they reveal, in order to see that the tripartite core of the analytical method – dream analysis, transference analysis, resistance analysis – was already shaped, and that the 'Fragment' is its methodological manifesto.

In the work of analysis of the two dreams we see the virtuoso at work, more in the skill with which he elicits his associations (such as the brilliant recognition that Dora had given him two weeks' notice – secretly – like a servant) than in the imagination with which he sorts and collates the material that is produced. He is already a master at recognising equivocation, evasiveness, gaps in the material, 'switch words', allusions to childhood (cf. an 'accident in the night'= bedwetting), verbal linkages, puns, visual imagery (the brilliant realisation that the reference to the painting of nymphs in a wood symbolizes the female genitals, the labia minora or nymphae among the pubic hair). But, as with Breuer and Anna O., we must give some of the credit to Dora, for she seems to have been a superb patient, another analyst manqueée, so that we are prone to join with Freud in regretting that his as yet inadequate technique for dealing with the transference did not enable her to curb the impulse to *act out* (the first reference to what was later conceptualised in the paper on transference) what Freud called the 'new edition' or 'revised edition' of her infantile relation to her father. If he had been both identified with and a little in love with Elisabeth von R., Freud was surely now finally in love with the method that was carrying him forward. We see the poet, rather than the neurophysiologist, formulating images of symptoms woven around an incident, as a pearl is formed around a grain of sand, or thoughts weaving themselves around an event like garlands of flowers around a wire.

It cannot have escaped notice, and may have caused some irritation, that in these chapters I have spoken little about the various stages of Freud's thought on the nature of hysteria, his psychopathological theories. I have not done so because, first of all, they are laid out beautifully in the papers and annotated splendidly by Strachey, and secondly, I do not regard them as greatly important in themselves. But I do wish to spend a little time reviewing the evolution of Freud's thought about psycho-pathology in general, and hysteria in particular, in a way that is somewhat different from that of the discussion in Chapter 1 concerning his modes of thinking, preconceptions, and model building.

The field which Freud entered with Breuer's help was one dominated by concepts which set psychopathology apart from normality on an underlying assumption of damage to the brain. This engendered terms such as 'degeneracy', assumptions of 'hereditary taint', suspicion of congenital or acquired syphilis, or dismissal as malingering. The Freud of the *Project* could take no other view despite his work, already six years old, with Breuer. These ideas of 'brain' had in that publication already yielded their place as 'specific aetiology' to one of 'predisposition'. Although Freud never fully embraced Breuer's idea of the 'hypnoid state' as the precondition for the formation of hysterical symptoms, and finally abandoned it openly in the 'Fragment', it is clear from his letters to Fliess, as late as the writing of the 'Dora' case record, that he had not yet given up the idea of 'organic factors'. These however had become attached to the biochemical processes he assumed lay behind bisexuality (one must remember, hormones had not yet been discovered). When he wrote in 1896 of the 'specific aetiology' of hysteria as a traumatic seduction in child-hood, he still meant this to be imposed upon some organic sexual predisposition in order for hysteria to appear in later life. It is probably correct to say that Freud never fully freed himself from the neurophysiological nor the biological view of predisposition, but he clearly abandoned the concept of brain for one of mind in committing himself as a 'psychologist' . The term 'metapsy-chology' with its four-part structure, only appeared in 1915 with the publication of 'The unconscious' (*SE* XIV), but if we examine these earlier writings on psychopathology in the light of topog-raphy, dynamics, economics, and genetics, we can see – albeit in a sort of swirling confusion – that Freud's theoretical views were already sorting themselves out under these four categories.

I have tried to indicate that the split between the clinician and the theoretician which Freud himself noted and referred to as the 'short story' quality of his clinical reports, was dissolving by the time the 'Fragment' was published. He was clearly thinking of Dora's personality, character, temperament, interests, phanta-sies, longings, as well as her conflicts. She comes out to us as a person in a manner which makes human such theoretical terms as 'splitting-of-consciousness', 'defence', 'inadmissable ideas'. The topography of levels of consciousness had already been put forward as universal in the three volumes *Traumdeutung*, *Wit*, and *Everyday Life*. Furthermore, the 'unconscious' (for Freud had already abandoned on the one hand the alternative term 'subconscious' to differentiate his views from the hypnotists, and the term 'the repressed' as too narrow) is presented as a realm of mental activity and not as a sub-cellar of rejected ideas and forgotten experience. Even hints of the structural ideas of the 20s are adumbrated in reference to multiple personality orga-nizations, as Breuer also noted with Anna O. (or rather as she noted to him). 'Stratification' of memories in 'at least three differ-ent ways', 'files of memories', and other ideas of a structural order in the mind are sprinkled through the theoretical sections.

Dynamic concepts include 'defence', the relation of mind and body through 'symbol formation' and 'somatic compliance', the use of one relationship to ward off another, the 'projec-tion' of ideas, the function of dreams to 'link the past and the present', of words to 'hold experience in consciousness', and many others. The idea of 'trauma' was broadening into one of 'cumulative experience' and 'over-determination'. The economics of the mind still held a quantitative hydrostatic, 'energetic' mode of exposition through the idea of 'cathexis'; but the attempt to distinguish between motives, reasons, tendencies, impulses, aims, object choice, choice of neurosis, the balance between progression and regression, and other ways of formulating the problems of quality – were pushing the more physical and neurophysiological models into the background. The genetic category was firmly entrenched in the *Three Essays* and the 'Fragment'. Clearly the hope of a 'complete analysis' was being given up, as it depended heavily on the idea of trauma as the ultimate cause of a pathological chain of events. 'Proof' was giving way to 'understanding' and the therapeutic power of analysis could no longer be attributed to the impingement of the analyst on the patient, but must wait for the patient to make use of the realizations that the analyst has made available. The humility of the first psychoanalyst was a far cry from the domineering and demanding psychotherapist of the *Studies*.

It will be recalled that in speaking of Freud's work, I emphasised the necessity for following the essential split in his functioning as a scientist: a split which can be fairly clearly defined as dividing the theoretician from the clinician. Here I wish to investigate with you the application of this conception of his mode of work to the evolution of dream interpretation. Throughout the length of Freud's 50 years of work as a psychologist, his attitude towards dreams, from the theoretical point of view, never really seems to have shifted from the early preconceptions expressed in the *Project*, and the theoretical ideas expressed in the famous seventh chapter of the *Interpretation of Dreams*. The central idea of this conception was that dreams were a rather simple mental function with a very simple purpose: namely, to keep the dreamer asleep; and that whatever was of interest about dreams was of interest not because of their meaningfulness in mental life, but because of what they could inadvertently reveal to the psychoanalyst. This essentially trivial function of dreams was seen as being implemented by means of a process akin to hallucination; and its effectiveness in keeping the dreamer asleep was based on a process of wish-fulfilment through hallucination.

Freud describes that his interest in dreams was really aroused in the course of the early work with hysterical patients, when he was still following Breuer's technique of catharsis and tracing symptoms back to their origins. He discovered that in the place of events, or occurrences, or thoughts, the patients did occasionally tell him dreams that had occurred. From this he construed that it was technically legitimate for him to treat the dreams as if they were 'thoughts like any other thought', but not to treat the dreams theoretically as if they were arranged in a continuous chain of mental process. Instead he conceived of them as being essentially concocted by an elaborate process in which wishes were granted fulfilrnent in a hallucinatory form, with the proviso that they sufficiently disguised themselves either to meet the requirements of an internal censorship, or 'cleverly' to evade this censorship.

Freud therefore tended to consider the manifest content of the dream as being patent nonsense, while the latent content of the dream − or the dream-thought and its significance − had to be construed in a piecemeal fashion − what he called the 'jigsaw puzzle' method. Taking each part of the dream in sequence and eliciting its associations, which then had first to be translated by means of the analyst's recognition of the dream work that had taken place, the analyst could then translate the assembled parts back to its 'original form', as it were, prior to the dream work that was dedicated to the evasion of the censorship. They could then be fitted together to produce the 'dream thought' whose significance could then be construed. The dream interpretation, as he says in a later paper on the technique, can therefore be divided into two phases: the first a phase essentially of translation; the second a phase of interpretation; and he likens it to translating a passage of Livy into German. This is of course a commentary on the kind of schooling he himself had, assuming that translation should naturally fall into these two phases: firstly translating from the Latin word to the German literal word, and then construing the propositional meaning and expressing this in literary or colloquial German. The teaching of language today, even of ancient languages, is in rebellion against this cerebral method − and so I would think is the approach to the interpretation of dreams.

Therefore in summary one might say that Freud treated dreams as if they were intrinsically useless artefacts of mental functioning with only the trivial function of keeping the dreamer asleep; and that it was the fact that the psychoanalyst could make use of them which elevated them to a position of importance in mental life. This was his theoretical position; and of course one might say that the yield of scientific data that he reaped from dreams under the aegis of this theory was very considerable indeed. He did construe from what he felt were 'wishes' (which I think we can take to mean some thing like the primitive impulses combined with rather omnipotent means of effecting the desires) something of the mental mechanisms by which people deceive themselves; and this, you might say, was gradually evolving into the theory of the mechanisms of defence. Certainly he construed something of the affects and passions that lay hidden in the depths of the mind and which were suggested or sometimes seen quite openly in the dreams. But on the other hand, the method in practice, and the yield from applying the method in practice, was vastly greater than the yield seen through the eyes of the theoretician.

In practice he treated the dreams as life events. For instance in the famous case of the 'Wolf Man', he has clearly implied that the most crucial event in this man's life occurred at the age of four when he had this particular dream of the wolves sitting in the tree. And probably most important of all, though something of which we know very little, Freud did utilize his own dreams to conduct his self-analysis following the deterioration of his relationship with Breuer and the collapse of the theory of the 'specific aetiology' of hysteria, which he had put forward in 1896. The collapse of his hopes of fame together with the death of his father at this time probably threatened him with the collapse of his mental health; and where others undoubtedly would have taken refuge in external flight, Freud turned inward, utilising his method to conduct his self-analysis, which seems to have been one of the most successful analyses in history.

We have many glimpses into this self-analysis in his *Interpretation of Dreams*, because Freud used many of his own dreams to illustrate his points there. But the clearest of all and the most revealing, owing to the wealth of associative material which he presents with it, is the famous 'dream of Irma's injection'. You will recall that this is essentially a dream in which he meets this patient, Irma, who complains to him that his treatment of her has not succeeded, and he replies that it is her own fault because she has not accepted his solution, and there follow various interactions between her and his friends Otto and Leopold, who examine her. It is of special interest that this dream is presented as an example of the method for interpreting dreams, and is preceded by a preamble in which Freud specifically abandons what he calls the 'popular' methods: that is the use either of inspiration or of decoding. Now it is true that by these two popular methods he means something like the extremes of a continuum, with inspiration at the one end and decoding at the other. 'Inspiration' would be a procedure by which the interpreter simply 'knows' the meaning of the dream without having to give any thought to it, without having to collect any information about the dreamer or the circumstances of the dream. Whereas the method of decoding would be a rigidly mechanical system of fixed-symbol translation of the Dream Book variety. It would not involve any element of interpretation of the significance of the dream (and analogously, the method of inspiration would pay no attention at all to the individual details of the dream). In presenting his own method, Freud does not give the impression that he is offering a method which lies somewhere in between these two extremes, but rather claims that he is following an entirely different method. If anything, he seems to see his method as closer to the decoding, if only because he takes his material in detail and not 'en masse', as he says. But his claim is that in following the elements of the dream into their associative connections in the patient's mind through free association he is able to determine the individual meaning of the symbols, rather than by relying on some form of standard dream-book decoding. It is therefore the function of inspiration that he primarily eschews.

I wish now to turn to two examples of Freud's work with dreams in practice: the specimen dream of Irma's injection, and the first in the 'Fragment of a case of hysteria': Dora's dream of the jewel-case; in order to examine the question whether these three claims have any validity: the claim that he is examining a process whose only function is to keep the dreamer asleep; that he is avoiding the use of inspiration, but rather relying on a purely inductive method of collecting items of information from which he then draws out scientifically valid conclusions. I believe that Freud at that time was very concerned with scientific respectability, trying to establish not only his own but also that of psycho-analysis as a method. We are talking of a time when the concept of scientific procedure as inductive was in great force in Germany, probably mainly on the basis of Emmanuel Kant's conceptions of apriori thought as an extension of experience. It was only beginning to be questioned, or rather to cause serious disturbance in scientific circles, following the work of David Hume and Poincaré and others who took the view that the idea of induction was a kind of self-idealisation, with the scientist really denying the extent to which he was avoiding looking at those other phenomena which might not substantiate the conclusions that he had reached by the inductive method of generalising his limited experience. The difficulty in Freud's thought resides, as it still resides in psychoanalysis, in not recognising that the procedures that could be considered scientific when dealing with the inanimate world are not only somewhat delusional when it comes to dealing with animate matter; but quite beyond possibility where mental processes are concerned.

When we examine the analysis of the 'specimen dream', we find that Freud does as he promises: faithfully takes the dream bit by bit and gives his association for each part. This goes on for ten pages, and then suddenly we are confronted by the statement: 'I have now completed the interpretation of the dream'. We are astonished to read this, but he goes on to say: 'While I was carrying it out, I had some difficulty in keeping at bay all the thoughts that were bound to be provoked by comparison between the content of the dream and the concealed thoughts lying behind it. And in the meantime the meaning of the dream was borne in upon me.' We are to understand therefore that the interpretation of the dream is something different from the construing of its meaning; and Freud summarises the meaning of the dream as follows:

> The dream fulfilled certain wishes which were started in me by the events of the previous evening: the news given me by Otto and my writing out of the case history. The

conclusion of the dream, that is to say, was that I was not responsible for Irma's pains, but that Otto was.'

He then goes on to expand on this, and within two pages comes to what seems to be a very different conclusion:

The group of thoughts that played a part in the dream ena-bled me retrospectively to put this transient impression into words. It was as though he (Otto) had said to me: 'You don't take your medical duties seriously; you are not conscientious, you don't carry out what you have under-taken.' Thereupon this group of thoughts seemed to have put itself at my disposal, so that I could produce evidence of how highly conscientious I was and how deeply I was concerned with the health of my relations, my friends and my patients.

Let us turn away for a minute from Freud's theoretical conclu-sions and discuss what we ourselves seem to learn from read-ing this dream and the wealth of associated material that Freud produces for it. We learn that we are dealing with an ambitious young man who had already made some fairly reckless experi-ments with cocaine that had resulted in deaths; who is worried that he is now engaged on another reckless experiment, and that his friends are turning against him. We discern behind this that he is troubled by his sexual interest in his women patients, and by his dependence on some of his men friends and their good opinion of him: most importantly on Dr M. We are given many indications that he is restless and uneasy in his marriage and dissatisfied with his sexual relationship with his wife and feel-ing guilty about difficulties in her health. We also learn that he is rather hypochondriacal himself, and still suffering from the consequences of deaths close to him. We also get a very clear indication that in the nebulous field of psychology he finds himself longing for the greater precision of biochemistry and anatomy. Therefore we would say that the extensive view of the inner life of the person Freud here afforded to us by the wealth of association gives a very different impression from the rather cold medical-student competitive atmosphere of the manifest content of the dream. Now I think one must realise that this is a dream of Freud's self-analysis and it therefore does not contain the structure of condensed transference significance that one might reasonably expect to find in the dream of a patient undergoing psychoanalysis. Its content and its associations roam freely over Freud's mental life at the time; even its fairly precise reference to the annoyance over the remark that Otto had made to him is only a starting point and not a real focus of the dream, as a similar remark by an analyst in his consulting room might be the focus for a patient's dream of the following night.

I would therefore suggest that examination of the dream does not at all bear out the method that Freud claimed to be following. I would suggest that the method he was following in practice was to use the dream as an entree into lines of association which revealed the person's unconscious mental life. What resulted from it has the structure of a short story (as Freud himself described his case histories}, rather than of a mathematical or scientific solution.

It is of interest, in line with Freud's self-analytic experience of these dreams, that, when we turn to the first dream of 'Dora' in the 'Fragment of a case of hysteria' we note that Freud took particular interest in the dream because it was presented by the patient as a repetitive one. That is, he does not seem to have taken interest in it as something referring to immediate events taking place in the analysis, but as something which could contribute to the reconstruction of the genesis of the patient's symptoms. This was natural because, although at the time he had discovered the functioning of the transference, he was considering it only to be a nuisance or an impediment and was making no effort to analyse it, even as a resistance. In the case of the 'Rat Man', Freud analysed the transference and its evolution for its own sake, but never considered it the premier method of psychoanalysis as we do today. The dream is short; I would like to present it as a unit:

'The house was on fire. My father was standing by my bed and woke me up. I dressed quickly. Mother wanted to stop and save her jewel-case, but Father said: "I refuse to let myself and my two children be burned for the sake of your jewel-case." We hurried downstairs, and as soon as I was outside I woke up.'

Dora's treatment occurred in the same year as the publication of the *Interpretation of Dreams*: 1900. The case history was written primarily as an addendum to the dream-book, rather than as a case to present Freud's views on the psychotherapy of hysteria. It seems to have been written very rapidly after the completion of Dora's brief treatment, and was at first called 'Dreams and hysteria': but its publication was then delayed for about four years for reasons that are not quite clear. It is clear from the work with Dora, however, that by this time Freud had given up directing the patient to follow the manifest content of the dream so carefully, piece by piece in producing associations, but gave Dora quite some leeway to follow her own bent. The associations which she produced and the ways in which Freud helped her to investigate these associations produce a wealth of interesting material about her relationship with Herr K., to her father and mother, to jewellery, and the early problem of bedwetting. In fact Freud does some symbol-translating on a purely inspirational basis: he translates jewel-case as vagina; he translates tear-drop earrings as semen.

At this point Freud is no longer referring to the interpretation of the dream and its meaning, for some reason; he seems to be referring to the analysis and the synthesis as the two phases of this process. But this synthesis takes some six pages to describe. The analysis had taken 25. Strangely enough, at the eighth page of the analysis we come to the astonishing statement as in the 'Irma' dream: 'Well, the interpretation of the dream now seemed to me to be complete.'

And in a footnote he says: 'The essence of the dream might perhaps be stated in words such as these: 'The temptation is so strong, father, protect me as you used to in my childhood and prevent my bed from being wetted.' With this banal and trivial statement we must compare the wealth of information and revelation about the life events, the temperament, the longings, the anxieties (and the relationship to Freud) that are revealed in this dream.

Freud did recognise that the dream recurred at this point in the analysis because it represented the repetition of a dangerous situation, and that she was experiencing the danger of sexual excitement and a sexual relationship to Freud as she had experienced it with Herr K. He did indeed come to regret that he had not dealt with this transference. It therefore seems reasonable to suggest that we have in the analysis of Dora's first dream an example of Freud the clinician using the dream, which is at considerable variance with Freud the theoretician talking about the function of the dream. It seems quite clear that he is using the dream as an entrée into the private, historical and emotional depths of the patient's mind, and from this material is also construing the immediacy of the unconscious situation in the transference. In theory what he is doing is tracing back Dora's hysterical symptoms to the kiss by the lake, and defining the nature of the mental mechanisms, denials, reversals, wishes and counter-wishes which underlie the formation of such hysterical symptoms.

In our tracing of the development of Freud's work we have now come to, say, 1904, just before the famous *Three Essays on Sexuality* and the 'Little Hans' case; we have covered the period of the *Studies on Hysteria*, the early elaboration of the theory of the defence neuropsychoses, the period during which Freud's explorations of the unconscious also produced the book on jokes, *The Psychopathology of Everyday Life*, and the great *Dream* book. I have been trying, by emphasising what the clinical evidence reveals of the way Freud actually *worked* with his patients, to show the considerable split between the clinician and the theoretician. I would remind you that the essential theme of this book consists really in tracing the way in which Freud, over the years, gradually metamorphosed from the determinist neuro-physiologist of the *Project for a Scientific Psychology* into the phenomenological psychologist of 'Analysis terminable and interminable'.

CHAPTER FOUR

Freud's theory of sexuality

W e must now try to investigate a subject that runs through all Freud's work, and is at the very heart of the psychoanalytic method and the psychoanalytic understanding of the mind: namely, the problem of sexuality. In approaching this, as in approaching other aspects of Freud's work, I want to try to differentiate between the method with its associated data, and the theories which are often strongly influenced by preconceptions; and to remind you that I have spoken of the way in which Freud was transformed from the determinist neurophysiologist into a phenomenological psychologist over the period of the forty years of his psychoanalytic work. Freud is probably best known for his revolutionary views on sexuality; but I think when we study them in practice we will be less inclined to consider them as revolutionary views and more inclined to see them as real discoveries. In order to make this differentiation it is necessary to read the *Three Essays* as laid out in the standard edition with great care, because it has been presented with a certain disingenuousness. Its format runs counter to the general format of the edition, which is chronological with cross-referencing. The editors for some reason have followed a different policy with the *Three Essays*. I wish to remind you, to begin with, of the way in which one must read it if one is to get a chronological idea in one's mind of Freud's development.

There were six editions of the *Three Essays* brought out in Freud's lifetime, beginning in 1905 and ending in 1926, of which four contain significant changes in his views: mostly additions, but also some corrections. The editors of the Standard Edition have for some reason chosen to present the last (1926) as the basic text and to annotate this with footnotes. The result is that one has the greatest difficulty in reading it chronologically, because it is very difficult to read something and then, on the basis of a footnote, to remove it from one's mind in order to gain an idea of what Freud thought in 1905. If they had wished to present a truly chronological picture for the student to grasp, they should have presented the first edition and footnoted it with the additions and subtractions of later editions. Therefore, to begin with, I want to outline the major alterations to the original 1905 edition (there are large sections which have as it were to be 'removed'); and then later go on to present a more integrated picture of Freud's views on sexuality in 1905. In Chapter 5 the ideas will be seen in action in the work with Little Hans. The main parts which have to be removed are the section on pregenital organization (which came only in 1915) and the section on the sexual researches of children, which came in the 1910 edition. This latter includes the description of the Libido Theory and various changes in his description of object choice and the basis of perversions. Finally the views about the physiological basis of sexuality (that is the hormonal theory) were merely a speculation in the 1905 edition and could not reasonably of course have been based on scientific research until about the 1920s.

With these additions and other minor changes, it seems to me that Freud's views on sexuality remain virtually the same throughout his career. This is perhaps particularly surprising when we consider that the *Three Essays* are presented as being based primarily on information available to any practitioner of medicine, modified and in a sense limited by the interests and findings of psychoanalysis as far as it had progressed by 1905. The later editions show the modifications and findings that psychoanalysis could subsequently introduce to it. In presenting an ordered picture of Freud's views on sexuality, I am going to use a format which is quite different from that which he follows in his own presentation, which was primarily organised around the psycho-analytic problem of the explanation or exploration of aberrations of sexuality. Therefore Freud naturally starts with these aberrations, and only then goes back to the description and investigation of infantile sexuality and the developmental transformations of puberty. I want to follow a more developmental sequence, starting with the infantile sexuality, and then describing Freud's views on the psychopathology of sex. At first, Freud seemed to have a preconception in his mind which one might call a rudimentary field theory of sexual behaviour. It consisted of dividing the determinants of sexual behaviour into three categories: the source of the sexual impulse, the aim of the sexual impulse, and the object of the sexual impulse. The concept of 'source' was more or less co-extensive with the concept of 'instinct', taking the view that the bodily organs developed tensions which required release, and that these tensions clustered around what Freud was calling the 'erogenous zones'. A few years later, in 1910 or 1915, he was inclined to extend this, to view everything on the surface of the body as capable of erogenicity; but still his view was that the primary erogenous zones were the genitals, the anus and the mouth. To this he added certain other functions or tendencies which he called the 'component instincts'. These he placed in a position of dependence upon experience for their mobilisation. Thus, for instance, the component instincts essentially consisted of voyeurism, exhibitionism, sadism and masochism. His view was that these component instincts were not necessary or physiologically based tendencies, but were latent tendencies called into play by the events in the child's life, which seemed to mean fundamentally by seduction or by example. The sexual instinct was therefore viewed as a bodily function that was essentially meaningless, finding its meaning only through the later elaboration of its connection with objects. His view therefore was that the relief of these tensions was a meaningless and auto-erotic activity until a certain period when object-seeking began. In his earliest views, this period of object-seeking does not seem to have commenced until somewhere around the third year, when the genital zone imposed its primacy on the sexual life. This implies that the earlier periods – those occupied with oral cravings and anal tensions – were fundamentally auto-erotic, meaningless, and did not in themselves contribute memories. They were not subject to the inhibitions due to conflict, and were therefore not sources of anxiety. They were not subject to repression and did not give rise to symptom formation. His view was that only with the rising of the genital primacy and the object-seeking of the genital tension did the Oedipus complex evolve, which placed the child in conflict in relation to its genital yearnings; that this conflict produced inhibitions; that these inhibitions functioned as dams to the flow of the sexual libido; and that when this flow of sexual energy or libido was blocked, it filled up what he called the 'collateral channels' of the pregenital impulses connected with orality and anality and the component instincts.

Therefore, in this earliest time Freud considered that the sexuality of children, of an oral and anal sort, was something that was hardly detached from the general reservoir of instincts serving self-preservation; and that they more or less detached themselves and assumed the status of a separate organisation of instincts, only when object-seeking and the Oedipus complex and conflicts relating to it arose, somewhere around the third year. Now, of course one does not know whether to call this a theory, or a model, or a mode of thought. I think probably it is more useful to think of it as the model or mode of thought that was most natural to Freud, natural to his era. It has been called the 'hydrostatic' model of instincts and mental functioning; and is based on a conception of there being a homogeneous excitation, equivalent in the body to the pressure of water or the voltage in an electrical system. It flows, has direction, and operates in time. It is subject to various kinds of interferences in this flow and therefore resorts to various types of distribution. Only when object-seeking enters into the picture are the activities related to sexuality seen as being meaningful, and it is only when they become meaningful that they are subjected to elaboration and phantasy and can enter upon a developmental process which can be thought of as essentially mental. It is only in this latter development that emotions and affects can be seen to play a part. It is a great weakness in Freud's model that it gives no scope for affects as qualitative factors in mental life, but necessarily reduces them to the status of a variable quantity of excitation; apprehended *as if* there were qualitative differences.

On the basis of this model of the auto-erotic phase, Freud discerned {or perhaps it was inherent in his model that this should exist) a certain gradient or differentiation between active and passive aims. This differentiation between active and passive aims of the instinct was seen by him as a foundation for the later establishment of tendencies which could be clearly delineated as masculine and feminine. He seems to have quite unequivocally considered masculinity to be essentially active and femininity to be essentially passive. But it is important to realise that he is not talking about modes of activity for the realisation of these aims (for he knew very well that a passive aim could be actively implemented and an active one could be passively implemented), but nonetheless in the realm of aims of the sexual instinct, this distinction seemed certain to him: that masculinity had active aims and femininity passive ones. I think one has to take it as a cultural aberration, or a preconception that was so ingrained in his times as to be un equivocally fixed in his mind. It is quite incompatible with his attitude towards orality, for instance; he did not see orality as essentially passive. It also had implications for his views about the little girl's relation to her body, for it would seem to have been (on some mysterious kind of negative evidence) that little girls knew nothing of their vaginas; they knew only of their clitoris and their rectum. His view was therefore that little girls suffered from a sense of weakness and helplessness and inferiority in the genital area, and perhaps an inbuilt sense of guilt as if the smallness of their clitoris-penis was tantamount to evidence of their having already been punished for some crime or sin. 'Penis envy', as he called it, seemed therefore to be the most natural phenomenon in the world, while a corresponding masculine envy of femininity could not be formulated since the existence of the female organ and the functions implied were not seen to play a role in the life of children. This seems to have remained virtually unchanged throughout his work, though Freud later recognised that sexual development in the girl has special difficulties connected with it, primarily those related to the strength of her primary attachment to the mother and the difficulty this posed in turning to the father in her oedipal conflict.

By 1915 the phenomenon of narcissism came within Freud's purview and was inserted between auto-eroticism and object relatedness in his view of the development of the libido. But while this opened for view a new range of clinical phenomena, it had little impact on his basic ideas on sexuality, developmentally speaking; although his attitude towards sexual pathology was certainly altered from that either stated or implied in the 1905 edition. There the sexuality of the child was characterised as 'polymorphously perverse', by which he meant subject to dissemination throughout the erogenous zones and only poorly under the domination of the genital. On this basis he could say that neuroses were the negative of perversions, brought about by inhibiting forces which were seen to originate mainly in the milieu, especially in the attitudes of the parents.

The central anxiety situation, castration anxiety, was a puzzle, as it might have had its inception from a threat connected with masturbation (Little Hans, the Rat Man), or from the perception of the differences between the anatomy of the genitalia of the sexes. This latter was seen as certain to be perceived as a mutilation, in boys and girls alike. Only with the analysis of the Rat Man did a purely internal conflict (between love and hate) take its place as a source of castration anxiety, and again in the Wolf Man (between masculinity and femininity).

This simple view of the relation of perversions to neuroses characterised Freud's theory until the Wolf Man revealed to him something of the complexity of perversity; how it was compounded of ambivalence, sado-masochism, fetishistic trends and passivity, all generating regression of the libido to pregenital points of fixation. In 1905 his view of the perversions was that they were simple, uninhibited actings of infantile sexual impulses, including the component instincts, while homosexuality was seen as primarily a matter of object choice, based on developmental experiences. The advent of a concept of narcissism and beginning recognition of the complex role of identification processes in development brought a sweeping change.

But what perhaps never changed was Freud's instinct-bound attitude towards sexuality: that its essential function was the relief of sexual tension, upon which biological function and meaningful object relations might be superimposed. For this reason, since this biological drive was seen to exist mainly in the male in connection with his constant production of semen, women were considered relatively asexual. Their biological drive was for children and it was to their children that their sexual love was given. How all this was compatible with the immaturity of the genitals in children, while nonetheless their sexuality was being insisted upon, is a little mysterious. However, this is perhaps one more area in which a split may be discerned between the clinician and the theorist. The case of Little Hans does not seem to bear out these basic concepts, but rather shows a little boy struggling with his love and hate, desire for knowledge, sadistic trends, and certainly his feminine as well as his masculine oedipal conflict. Freud, the clinician, even suspected that exposure to the primal scene played some role in his illness, an idea he brought to the attention of his followers only some thirteen years after the publication of the case of Little Hans, in the famous Wolf Man dream from which Freud reconstructed an event of exposure to parental coitus at the age of eighteen months.

In this chapter therefore, as an introduction to the case of Little Hans, which was written as an addendum to the *Three Essays* (as was 'Dora' to the *Traumdeutung*) I have tried to pull together Freud's views on sexuality as they existed in 1905, in order to rectify the confused chronology which a reading of the Standard Edition tends to impose upon one.

CHAPTER FIVE

The case history of Little Hans (the infantile neurosis)

The case of Little Hans was published in 1909 only a few months before the publication of the Rat Man case. The clinical work on both these patients had taken place one year before this and the case of the Rat Man had in fact commenced some months prior to Freud's starting work with Little Hans' father to resolve the child's phobia. This case history stands in relation to the *Three Essays on Sexuality* much as the Dora case stands in relation to the *Traumdeutung:* namely, as a clinical addendum to the theoretical publication and intended to illustrate the theory in action in the process of psychoanalytic therapeutic work. However, the publication of the Little Hans material had more meaning for Freud than merely that of a clinical exemplification of the theory in action; for it also signified a certain vindication (and, in a sense, proof of the truth) of his theory about infantile sexuality and of the existence of the infantile neurosis. Freud seems to have looked upon the opportunity of supervising the father's treatment of his child as something extraordinary and some thing whose frequent repetition could be little hoped for, since he could not envisage this sort of work being carried on by anyone other than a child's parent. In retrospect, this may seem rather peculiar to those who have grown quite accustomed to the treatment of children. In fact, the absolute opposite may seem to be true today. I am always rather surprised, however, that children will tolerate psychoanalytic treatment by anybody but their parents and find the evident ease with which little Hans confided his phantasies, acted out his hostility, recounted his dreams, and included Freud as the professor who was supervising his father – indeed the ease with which the whole process was contained within family life – highly impressive, but reasonable.

To review the content of the case briefly: you will recall that some years previously, Freud had asked people whom he called 'close adherents' (among whom were the parents of Little Hans) to send him observations illustrating the sexual researches of children. While he was in fact unable to obtain any information from the parents as evidence of the impact upon children of witnessing the primal scene (which I think was his particular interest), he continued to suspect very strongly that this factor was operative. After all, Little Hans had spent the first four years of his life in his parents, bedroom, including six months following the birth of his baby sister Hannah; and the event of being moved out of the bedroom for the night in order to allow his mother to give birth to Hannah, of coming back into the room and seeing bowls that were still filled with bloody water and so on, seems to have made a great impression on him. In any case, during the summer after the birth of Hannah, when the family stayed at the Gmunden resort, Hans' sexual life seems to have blossomed and his association with other children took on the colouring of his calling them 'his children.

Now Freud apparently viewed this, not as evidence of his femininity and identification with his mother, but rather as his way of compensating himself for the loss of his mother's attention; and it is this tendency on Freud's part, namely to diminish the significance of the boy's femininity in favour of the role of his masculine castration complex in the formation of his Oedipus conflict, which seems to be the chief weakness in the interpretative work. It might be attributed to a theoretical preconception of Freud's, or perhaps to a lack of differentiation between homosexuality and femininity in a male child. For although he does briefly talk about the homosexual implications of Hans' attachment to his father, he seems reluctant to leave the impression that Hans' sexual tendencies were what at that time would have been considered 'degenerate'.

To return: the incidents at Gmunden, which included such things as a little girl being warned not to go near a horse for fear he might 'bite her finger', and a little boy falling down after kicking a rock and his foot bleeding, seem to have mobilised a certain amount of castration anxiety in Hans. This gradually overcame him in subsequent months and produced an inhibition (or what Freud calls a repression) of his sexual impulses. These impulses had expressed themselves firstly in masturbation (for he had by now been moved out of his parents' bedroom and seems to have masturbated in the mornings or during his afternoon naps) and secondly, in an inhibition of his previously enthusiastic voyeurism and exhibitionism, of his interest in urine and faeces – for which he now showed a revulsion. It is of special interest that the record includes observations on the child's sexual development that the father had sent to Freud prior to the outbreak of the neurosis, so that we have some fairly accurate information upon which to construct the genesis of the illness. Anyway, Hans fairly suddenly developed a fear of going out of the house which he formulated as a fear of being bitten by a horse; and it is for this reason that Freud considered it a phobia. However, it seems clear from the development of the treatment after its prompt start, that the fear of being bitten by a horse was superficial compared to the agoraphobic aspect of the illness: that is, the fear of going out lest he encounter horses, particularly horses drawing heavily-laden carts, who might fall down and make a row with their legs. This central fear was connected with his own behaviour when told to go and sit on the toilet to defaecate; with the incident of the child who hurt his foot; and almost certainly, Freud thought, with observations of the primal scene. It evolves quite clearly that the heavily-laden carts represent the pregnant mother in particular; and that underlying the agoraphobia and anxiety state is Hans' great curiosity about conception and birth, about which he had been given no accurate information, but had been fobbed off with the stork story.

The development of the father's treatment of Hans under the careful supervision of Freud is fascinating and laid out in what might be called a perfect exposition of clinical work. It is undoubtedly the most delightful piece of writing in the whole of psychoanalytic literature, and every reading of it is of interest, not only because one sees new things in it each time, but because it is, after all, the prelude to child analysis. In a certain way, one is always inclined to feel that Freud drew much less of interest from this rich material than it actually contained. But this was not entirely a matter of blindness to the significance of clinical phenomena; it was also owing to the fact that Freud was interested in a limited exposition with reference to infantile sexuality and the evidences in favour of the existence of an infantile period of neurosis that was subsequently repressed and forgotten, forming the basis for a reappearance in adult life of neurotic symptomatology. He is particularly interested in demonstrating, through Little Hans' material, the reality of bisexuality, the reality of the genital and pregenital drives and interests of children; the reality of the castration complex, of the Oedipus complex, the evidences in favour of traumatic factors in the institution of castration anxiety: such as, in this case, the mother's threat to cut off Little Hans' 'widdler' if he touched his penis. And perhaps most importantly, he demonstrates the evidence for the part played in the development of the child of the birth of the next sibling: that is, the way in which it aroused his sexual curiosity, burdened him with intense jealousy and envy; and, in this case of a baby of the opposite sex, confronted Little Hans with the evidences of genital differences.

Now you will remember that at this time and through most of his career until the paper on female sexuality in 1928, Freud maintained his own belief and his own interpretation of clinical evidence that the female genital was viewed by all children, male and female alike, as a mutilation. Freud interpreted the evidence of Little Hans' attitude towards Hannah's genital as confirmation of this, although I think it is fairly unconvincing. The area that is convincing, and that Freud somehow fails to put together well, is Hans' construing that the birth of the baby was a painful and dangerous thing, judging from the sight of the bloody water in his mother's bedroom after the delivery and from hearing his mother's moaning (which he called 'coughing') during the birth. This is borne out by two sections of the material in particular: by the dream about the plumber taking away the bathtub and putting a bore into Hans' stomach (which clearly seems to be a phantasy of impregnation that links with Hans' other phantasies about joining his father in going under the rope into a forbidden space, or breaking a window in the railway carriage). And secondly, it is seen in Hans' play with the doll that had the little squeaker missing from its navel, into which he put the mother's penknife and then tore the legs open to extract the knife. Thus he illustrated his phantasy that something both penetrated into his mother in a painful way and something came out of her in a painful way that produced the bleeding. Freud had a very clear recognition of the fact that this sadistic concept of the creation of the baby played some part in Hans' sexual feeling toward his mother; particularly as expressed in his acknowledged desire to beat his mother in the way the coachman beat the horse.

The aspect of the case that is so fascinating to us as we read it today (and in which Freud took no special interest because, as I suggested before, it was not in line with what he wished to demonstrate), is the development of the treatment of the child. This starts with the purely phobic element: the fear of being bitten by the horse; goes on suddenly from that to the material about defaecation, the 'lumph' material; then moves quickly, by way of the sadistic element, into the material about the stork box and the birth of Hannah. From there the development moves to the phantasies about Hans' relationship to Hannah before she was born and, by implication, before he was born, when they lived together in the stork box. It is perhaps disappointing to us to see Freud treat this material in a rather trivial way and to view it as a means that Hans had of pulling his father's leg and having revenge on him for the lies he had been told about the stork. Freud overlooks, not the fact that it represents a phantasy about the mother's womb, but the fact that it is a problem to Hans: a problem of, as it were, life before conception: the child's difficulty in coping with the painful realisation that there was a time before he existed at all. Children are of course inclined to deny this in favour of the phantasy that they always existed inside their mothers; and of course, she must have always existed inside her mother, and she inside her mother, Russian-doll fashion back to the beginnings of time; and therefore also extrapolating into the future. The child has inside him babies who contain babies, who contain yet more babies ad infinitum. This aspect of the child's interest in the inside, its own inside and the inside of the mother in particular, does not seem to have attracted Freud's interest at all at this point. And it is in a sense quite different from his lack of interest in Hans' femininity. For it seems to me that he noted the evidences of his femininity but was reluctant to discuss or emphasize them. He therefore speaks very little of the feminine component in Hans' illness, namely, the one that came from his rivalry and envy of his mother and her capacity to have children, her capacity to be the father's wife and to receive his penis (or whatever Hans imagined she did that was represented by the penknife being put into the doll or the plumber putting the bore into Hans' stomach).

To turn away slightly from the actual case material and its virtues and deficiencies, back to its link with the *Three Essays on Sexuality*, it is perhaps important to remember that the way in which this piece of work is presented in the Standard Edition is somewhat difficult to read. Therefore one reads about narcissism, about the sexual researches of children, about masochism and perversions, in a way that only came to Freud much later in his work and thinking. In 1905, the formula that neurosis was the opposite of perversions was a very satisfactory one to him. It may seem somewhat odd that at the time when he was realising how complicated neuroses were, he was still willing to consider that perversions were very simple: the putting into action of the infantile 'polymorphously perverse disposition'. We must also remember that by 'polymorphously perverse', Freud was referring to the formulation of source, aim and object. His conception of perversity was exclusively joined to the concept of erogenous zones with the exception of what he called the 'component instincts' of scoptophilia, exhibitionism, sadism, and masochism. At that time he did not see these as necessary parts of sexual instinctual life, but as potential parts that could be aroused by stimulation or seduction from the outside. He also regarded homosexuality purely from the point of view of object choice. In the paper on Little Hans he comes very close to his later formulation of homosexuality as being related to a phase of narcissism. However, he does not call it narcissism here, but does say that it relates to something in the development that stands somewhere between auto-erotism and object relation.

With this simple formulation of the perversions in mind, Freud felt quite justified in defending them against what he considered to be public prejudice and in insisting that they were essentially benign; that the difficulties into which they ran were primarily social difficulties that forced repressions of the infantile impulse and that it was from these repressions (under the influence first of family pressures and later social pressures} that the damming-up of the libido ensued, to be followed subsequently by the conversion of the dammed-up libido into symptoms and anxieties.

Although the section of the *Three Essays on Sexuality* that deals with the sexual researches of children was not added until some years after the publication of 'Little Hans', it is fairly clearly indicated in this latter paper that Freud viewed these sexual researches as the prototype of children's curiosity about the world; and therefore, as the basis (when sublimated) of the thirst for knowledge. The implication at this point, then, is that the thirst for knowledge is driven by anxiety, and that knowledge will inevitably be used for defensive processes. It is perhaps worth noticing here that this is a very different view from the one Mrs Klein adopted – perhaps from her experience of listening to small children, rather than as a preconception. She found that there existed in them what she called the epistemophilic instinct': an instinctual thirst for knowledge and understanding; the first object of which was the child's mother, her body, and particularly (as the children told her) its inside. When we link this fact to Freud's experience with Little Hans, we can see that it was precisely this aspect of the child's phantasy that Freud was unable to recognize as significant and that the treatment ended before Hans could really investigate this area of his mental life with his father. The treatment ended because Hans seemed to have recovered from his symptomatology; and this, after all, was the therapeutic aim itself, and not as an adjunct to his character development. Therefore in looking forward to the significance of the Little Hans case for the development of child analysis, one is immediately struck with the difference in the work here with Little Hans and the work that Mrs Klein began in the 1920s. The work with Little Hans is essentially reconstructive and is aimed at an understanding of the pathology and therefore tends to look backwards on the child's life. Mrs Klein's work, on the other hand, is developmental from the very outset, and tends to look forward to the factors that are involved in the child's development. It is not psychopathological in its orientation.

In closing, it is perhaps important to mention that Freud goes to some lengths in his summing-up to plead the cause of the psychoanalytic method as not being dangerous to children: that is, it is not dangerous to arouse their sexual curiosity, to give them information, to relieve their repressions and arouse their interest in sexual subjects. This is certainly the slant of the post-script to the case, in which he reports a visit he had from Little Hans (aged nineteen) some fourteen years later, when he found that the boy had no memory of the events of his neurosis and that he was now a fine, strapping lad. While it may strike us as a little sad, it was apparently very heartening to Freud and was clearly taken as evidence that the work undertaken with him had not only helped him at the time, but had done no harm to his development. This plea is perhaps one that not all of us would absolutely endorse today: partly because we carry on much longer treatment processes that are considerably more searching and go much deeper; and partly because we treat children who are far more ill than Little Hans. He was not, after all, a fundamentally ill child; on the contrary he seems to have been eminently healthy, but to have developed a transient phobia as almost any child does at some time in his early years. I think that most child analysts today would feel that the investigation of a child's mental life, the opening-up of the stream of unconscious phantasies, the intrusion of a stranger into the close intimacy of the family, has many dangers.

In summary: the case of Little Hans is a useful clinical addendum to that part of the *Three Essays on Sexuality* that deals with infantile sexuality. It also illustrates very richly for us the quality of Freud's thought at this point and serves as an excellent prelude to the study of the work that he was writing almost simultaneously: namely, the Rat Man case, in which we will see that he makes some extremely important discoveries that are implicit in the Little Hans case but not explicitly stated. These are discoveries about the role of ambivalence, the interplay of love and hate in the formation of internal conflict. Up to this time, the concept of conflict in Freud's writing seems mainly to embrace the conflict between instinct and the outside world and the position of the ego as it tries to manage these conflicting interests under the sway of the pleasure principle.

CHAPTER SIX

The Rat Man (obsessional neurosis)

The case of the 'Rat Man' seems to have taken place in 1907, which means that it started before the treatment of Little Hans by his father under Freud's supervision. The Rat Man was in treatment for some eleven months before he himself broke it off, feeling well, able to face his exams, and to get on with his life. Freud reports in a footnote later that, like so many young men of promise, he died in the First World War. Not only is the paper itself of great interest, but we have also the extraordinary luck to have Freud's notes for the first four months, the notes that he made in the evening after he had finished his day's work. They are fascinating, and give us probably the most accurate picture that we have of Freud actually at work in his consulting room. Therefore we can attempt to draw some inferences from these notes with regard to Freud's technique, and to compare them with the technical papers that begin to appear some three or four years later.

We are perhaps struck by the way in which he starts the treatment, and in the first few sessions seems to give the patient a theoretical exposition of the method of psychoanalysis and its therapeutic rationale. Most striking perhaps is the contrast with the Dora case, for we see here that Freud was able to follow his patient almost to the exclusion of his seizing the initiative in pursuit of his own enquiries. This may be due partly to the fact that the material did tend to bubble forth from the Rat Man, and that the resistances fairly quickly turned into transference resistances, in which the patient described to Freud under great stress and distress, the phantasies he had of a sadistic and sexual nature toward him, toward his daughter, toward his mother, toward his family generally.

One notices the calmness with which Freud dealt with these transference manifestations; perhaps because of his theoretical orientation to them; viewing them, as he wrote about transferences, as new editions or re-editions of past events and relationships, which essentially had nothing to do with him personally. This is indeed an extremely useful attitude in dealing with the transference, but one may be inclined to think Freud adopted an aloofness towards the material which, while protecting him from countertransference involvement, may perhaps also have screened from himself the degree of his own emotional reaction to the patient's material and behaviour. There are not many instances that one would like to pinpoint as countertransference; the meal of herring that he served him does not seem to have been a breach of technique, for one suspects that Freud may have done this with patients quite regularly at that time. We must remember that there was not as yet a concept of countertransference. That only comes later, when Freud reports, around 1915, that he has become aware of the limitations of analysts: that they are limited by their perception of their own complexes and by the consequent countertransference. He is on the other hand troubled when he notices things that he can identify as breaches of technique or lapses in function such as when he felt uncertain as to whether a certain piece of material that he recollected did in fact belong to the Rat Man or was derived from some other patient.

The use that Freud makes of the transference is a little unclear; nor can we derive from his actual handling of it any idea of his attitude other than, as already noted, its being a repetition of past experience. He certainly seems to have derived information from it: that is, information from the transference that confirmed or refuted the formulations he was already deriving from the ordinary material of the patient's associations and recollections. One feels also that he perhaps derived a very special feeling of confirmation about reconstruction, in the same sense that, say, Little Hans' illness gave him a special confirmation of the existence of the infantile neurosis, the theory of which had been derived from the reconstruction of the material of adult neurotic patients. He does not seem to have viewed the transference as following any particular process in itself, nor to have made any attempt to follow it in its own right. He was probably dealing with it mainly as transference resistance, and allowing it to spend itself, while at the same time connecting its content with previous material.

Similarly, one may be disappointed to see how little he seems to have done with the many dreams that the Rat Man brought him, both current and past. There is nothing like the almost obsessive interest that he took in the Wolf Man's dreams some years later. And the analytic attention he does give the dreams in no way resembles the systematic jigsaw puzzle method he himself described. The comments on the dream of Freud's daughter with the dung over her eyes or the dream of the Japanese swords do not strike us as being particularly imaginative or penetrating.

From the point of view of therapeutic method, Freud seems still to have been following mainly the line of unravelling the history of the symptoms and their unconscious meaning. He does claim with some pride to have cleared up the main obsessions about the rat punishment. From the point of view of Freud's functioning in the consulting room one is very struck by the amount of fragmented and incomprehensible material that he seems to have been able to hold in his mind. If one had read (which unfortunately one seldom has) the notes before reading the paper, one would undoubtedly have experienced an overwhelming confusion about the material and then been utterly amazed by the way Freud has drawn it all together in his exposition. I would venture to say that there is very little in the notes which is not covered in the exposition; if not in the descriptive part, then later in the theoretical part. This seems quite amazing when you consider that the notes in our possession run to nearly the length of the paper itself. One must consider this a special aspect of Freud's genius: that he could allow so much disparate information to enter his mind and allow it gradually, very gradually, to become organized there. It is perhaps quite different from the usual picture that we have of Freud; of someone who had things highly organized in his mind and was always searching for confirmation of his theories. Perhaps the great virtue of this case history is that it shows us a side of Freud that we are not able to see in most of his writings: that is, Freud the phenomenologist. I think that one cannot but be filled with admiration at the minuteness of the details of his observation of character and character structure. I would think that most readers are rather bored by the lengthy exposition of the incident with the spectacles at the manoeuvres; and yet Freud was able to take an interest and to get all the details straight so that he could draw a map and knew exactly what transpired in this extraordinary incident of the paying back of the 3.8 kroner.

We see that he is able not only to pay minute attention to historical events of this sort but also to the phenomena that appear in the consulting room: the use of language, the patient's behaviour. He is for instance able to recognize immediately his patient being in a state of identification with his mother; able to recognize changes in mood and the evidence of emotionality of which the Rat Man was oblivious. One is struck by his non-judgmental attitude to this young man's sexuality and sexual behaviour; not only his phantasies but his relationships with women. One is inclined to think that some of Freud's revulsion was perhaps split off, as for instance when he gives an example not from the patient's material but from that of some other patient. (He reports that this man used to take the children of friends out into the country and when it would be too late to return by train, he would stay at a hotel and masturbate the girls. He was very offended when Freud asked him whether he didn't think this was dangerous.) Well, quite clearly Freud was shocked by this man's behaviour and not sorry to see him go away and not come back. But one feels that similarly he might have been a little shocked by the Rat Man's behaviour with his dressmaker, or perhaps most of all by his lack of feeling about the suicide of the earlier dressmaker, with whom he had had a prospective liaison; but that he kept his feeling about this at bay through his clinical detachment.

On the whole, Freud seems to have liked the Rat Man very well (though he does not come over to me as a particularly likeable person). Perhaps Freud's use of a concept of splitting and seeing the man as composed of three different personalities helped him to like the one that was most present to the world, the one that he calls affable. It is of interest to note that while he uses a concept of splitting of personality here as a way of explaining the nature of the psycho-pathology, it takes him another 25 years, to the paper on the 'Splitting of the ego in the service of defence', to take an interest in this process with regard to the question of mental health. It is an example of the extent to which Freud was a psychopathologist and how late in his career it was that he began to take an interest in the mysterious processes of mental health. Even in the Leonardo paper, which is perhaps the first paper in which Freud can be said to take an interest in a person as a whole, and a life as a whole integrated process, his interest in Leonardo's creativity is not taken as evidence of mental health of unusually fine quality, but as a manifestation of a particular kind of psychopathology that has been diverted through sublimation into useful social channels.

Freud's theoretical summing up of the Rat Man case is brilliant and beautifully organized. The most significant historical landmark is his establishment of the concept of ambivalence: a term that he says he borrowed from Bleuler. In the Rat Man he comes for the first time to a clear recognition of the conflict between love and hate as a possible basis for neurosis. This is very different from the notion of unacceptable ideas, for instance, which always implies a conflict with the outside world as the primary focus. Even castration anxiety, as expressed in Little Hans, is given an external world anchorage. If not in actual threats of mutilation by parents, it is anchored to the perception of the sexual difference in children: that is, to Hans' perception that his little sister did not have a 'widdler'. So this paper of the Rat Man presents a very great step forward in acknowledging internal conflict; conflict that is internal in its origin and not merely in its development.

The second landmark, which is perhaps more clearly discussed here than anywhere else in Freud's work, is the recognition of omnipotence. Freud describes it as omnipotence of wishes, and it gives us some clue as to why he felt that the wish was such an important factor in the dream. There is the brilliant description here of the elliptical use of language, and one can begin to grasp that he meant that a wish, particularly an omnipotent wish, was a desire that was operating elliptically to leap from its inception to its fulfilment. The use of the concept that he makes here is perhaps a little disappointing, in that he attributes importance to it only insofar as the patient appears to be frightened of his omnipotence. This would seem to imply that if he were not frightened of his omnipotence, it would not play any part in his psychopathology. On the other hand, he does link omnipotence to infantile development, and links it directly to what he calls the megalomania of childhood; although I must say that it is not at all clear to me what difference he wishes to draw between omnipotence and megalomania. The great analysis of obsessional doubting is probably the finest thing ever written about obsessionality. Freud's realisation that the doubting had its root in primal ambivalence and the formula that he educes that a man who doubts his love must necessarily doubt every lesser thing, is not only brilliant but poetically expressed. He has not apparently in this paper as yet forsaken his earlier formulation that obsessional neurosis had its roots in an active rather than passive sexual experience in childhood, but one can see that this formulation is weakened considerably in favour of locating the erotism as anal erotism and connected with sadistic, voyeuristic and exhibitionistic impulses.

So one might say that Freud had come at this point to a more complicated view not only of obsessional neurosis but of mental life in general. It is in keeping with this that his examination of the Rat Man's character strikes us as such an important advance and as a prelude to the examination of character which follows in later papers, such as the famous paper on anal erotism, on character types met with in analysis, and his investigation of the character of the Wolf Man. He writes in a very interesting way here about the attitudes towards death, superstition, and religion, of the obsessional neurotic. It seems reasonable to say that one of the advances marked by this case history from the point of view of the development of Freud's clinical thought is the way in which the concept of a child is beginning to flesh out, rather than being the bare schematic skeleton indicated in the *Three*

Essays on Sexuality. The evidences of Freud's awareness of the importance of identification processes; the recognition of divisions in the personality; the awareness of conflicts of love and hate and the role of omnipotence in infantile phantasy; all mark an advance in the complexity and richness of thought with regard to the commands that the Rat Man received. Some of these were dangerously destructive or self-destructive, such as the command to cut his own throat, or the command to kill the old woman. My impression is (though Freud does not state it explicitly) that he thinks these commands come from a deeply unconscious and very brutal part of the Rat Man's personality, and are directed to one of the two pre-conscious personalities: namely to the infantile polymorphously perverse part. I would think that in the development of his thinking in later years he would probably have viewed these commands as coming from a harsh superego, and this seems to be a problem of his later thought that has greatly exercised workers who have followed him. The confusion between narcissistic phenomena and sadism, or harshness, in the superego, is a problem that is far from resolved today.

Finally, let us note Freud's view of the role of masturbation in the genesis of the neuroses as expressed in this paper. One would say that it differs from that expressed in earlier papers on the defence neuropsychoses, or the aetiology of hysteria. One has the impression that Freud took a relatively benign view of the role of masturbation in earlier times and was inclined to view the absence of masturbation as an important item in determining the stasis of the libido and its being diverted into symptoms and anxiety. Here it seems more clear that he views masturbation as having some noxious influence on the life processes of the Rat Man, although it is not at all clear just how it operates. The impression is that as a substitute for sexual intercourse it is felt to be inadequate and somehow unsatisfying; but there are also indications that it brings him into conflict with the memory of his father, say, as represented in that particular piece of material where the Rat Man feels that his father is outside, knocking on the door; after he opens the door for him, he goes back into the house and looks at his genitals in the mirror – which Freud takes as a substitute for masturbation. So there is the beginning of a view that masturbation brings a child into conflict with an internal authority (the father) and in this way it is a prelude to Freud's later view on the role of the superego in promoting castration anxiety and neurotic conflict.

In summary, then, the case of the Rat Man represents a great advance in Freud's work in many directions: in the technical direction we see that his work with patients had become very committed to following the material rather than pursuing his own interests for the purpose of solving particular riddles of reconstruction. He seems to be making some use of transference phenomena, although it is not quite clear whether he is dealing with them as resistances only or also gathering important information from them. My impression is that he views these transference experiences as playing some role in the therapeutic process. From the phenomenological point of view, one sees a great advance in Freud's attention to mental phenomena, relatively unhampered by preconceptions of the sort expressed in the *Project for a Scientific Psychology.* Only at one point in the paper does he depart from phenomenological procedure and launch into a vast generalisation, and that is the part about the role of the sense of smell in the phylogeny of human beings, and the important role of sexuality in the genesis of neuroses. One is reminded that this way of theorising about a sense of smell has a link back to his former relation to Fleiss, which by this time (in 1909) was completely in abeyance. What are called the theoretical sections of the paper are indeed very phenomenological and trace with great clarity the meaning and the significance, from the unconscious point of view, of the patient's symptomology and character structure. The case of the Rat Man is therefore much more of a research paper than the other case histories, which are (on the contrary) more in the nature of expositions and demonstrations of existing theories.

CHAPTER SEVEN

The Leonardo paper (narcissism)

We have now reached 1910 and I want to spend this chapter on the Leonardo case. It is a paper I always used to dislike, although I have come to think better of it after re-reading it several times. I think that the reason I balked at it originally was that it is the beginning of a very bad tradition in psychoanalysis: Freud calls it a 'psycho-pathography', an investigation into the 'psycho-pathology of great men', and if one looks at it in that light it is a somewhat unpleasant thing. Although I believe most of the things he says about Leonardo are probably quite correct, and in a sense enlightening, I do not think it requires psychoanalytic insight to reach them. The aspect that is peculiarly psychoanalytic concerns the part about the bird putting its tail in the baby Leonardo's mouth, the preoccupation with the flight of birds, his flying machines, the supposed hidden vulture in 'The Virgin and Saint Anne' and similar material. Yet the writing is not good and to my mind is not really even interesting. Therefore I want to put aside this pathography aspect of the paper, which is the only one of its sort that Freud wrote and, in many ways, is one he apologises for and dissociates himself from at the end. However, one must remember that it is an important paper historically; the beginning of that extremely bad tradition in psychoanalytic writing which consists in scrutinising the private lives of great men by supposedly psychoanalytic methods from outside the psychoanalytic setting of the transference. I think it is boring and has probably done quite a lot of harm in particular to the relationship of psychoanalysis to the arts, since it is mainly artists and writers (and to some extent politicians and historical figures) who have received such treatment.

I want to consider now the important connection between Freud and Leonardo and the way in which the paper is auto-biographical. It is autobiography in that it relates to the split which I have been talking about from the very beginning of these chapters: namely, the split in Freud between the theoretician and the clinician. As I have stressed, the clinician in Freud is really an artist at work, and he does at many points in his life accuse himself of being artistic or poetic, of 'writing novels' and so on. Of this very paper he said that he was writing a psychoanalytic novel about Leonardo, and this is probably correct. However, I think that by this time in his life, the accusation of artistry, imagination and intuition did not worry him as much as it did at the beginning of his work. One can see that by this point there were really three Freuds fairly distinct from one another: Freud the artist-clinician, Freud the rather obsessional theoretician and builder of speculative systems that were supposed to be inductive theories; and thirdly, Freud the political leader, the Moses figure, concerned to start a psychoanalytic movement and keep it separate from medicine while at the same time appropriating much of the prestige and respectability from medicine: concerned also for it not to be a Jewish science while at the same time making terrific onslaughts on Christianity, as in this and in later papers (to an even fiercer degree). He was the kind of political leader who drove out deviants from the party line – such as Adler and Jung – whom he scourged over and over again in his writings, quite unnecessarily from the scientific point of view. Of these three quite distinct personalities of Freud, the really lovable one is to my mind the clinician: and it is he whom I wish to discuss.

It amuses me on reading the paper again to find that towards the end Freud described Leonardo as being at the 'summit' of his life when he was painting the Mona Lisa and having what Freud called 'renewed sexual drives': that is, when in his early 50s, which was Freud's age when he wrote the paper (54). For indeed it was in the Leonardo paper that the evolution of the concept of narcissism was first stated, the beginning of a new surge in Freud himself. Moreover, I believe the Leonardo paper is the beginning of a new attitude in Freud to psychoanalysis as something that investigates the whole person and his whole life. From that point of view, the pathography – the attempt to describe a whole person and his whole life – is really a very important effort on Freud's part. I am accordingly inclined to view it as amongst the case histories, although only derivatively in that it uses material from outside the analytic setting and is thus in the same class as, for instance, the Schreber case. It is not clinical work inside the consulting-room, but it is clinical thinking, and the data is drawn from literary work (mainly from Leonardo's notebooks and his paintings). Freud investigates Leonardo's life taking into accou nt what other people (as Vasari in his *Life*) have said about his paintings. It is an application of psychoanalytic thought to a certain type of data. And while one must naturally bear in mind that to try to draw out the life of a person from such shreds as these seems too ambitious when an analysis takes years and thousands of hours of careful listening, nevertheless the idea of trying to understand a whole person and his whole life – the idea of the psychoanalytic biography (as opposed to the idea of psychoanalytic pathography) is not in itself a bad one. It presents a new dimension for psychoanalytic thought. As I say, when it is applied to psychoanalytic scholarship, I do not like it; I think it is wrong and has initiated a bad tradition which includes that of psychoanalytic art criticism. This pays too much attention to the content in art and not enough attention to the more important formal aspects, which psychoanalysis is not really in a position to approach.

Therefore if we consider the paper as Freud's attempt to see psychoanalysis as a science which tries to understand the whole person and his whole life, and if we recognize that Freud, in his choice of Leonardo, is seeing something which is greatly troubling him about himself – namely the split between the investigator or what he called the 'Conquistador', and the artist – then we shall be going in a very important direction. We come up against the two most interesting aspects of the paper: the first being the discussion of the relation between the search for knowledge and emotionality; and this is a point of paramount importance with regard to the understanding of Mrs Klein's work. In preparation for this I will now spend some time investigating this last point about curiosity and the search for knowledge; its relationship to emotions, and particularly its relationships to love and hate. Towards the end of the chapter I will talk a little about the second interesting feature: namely, Freud's early and, in a sense, crude formulation of the concept of narcissism, which is also embodied in the paper.

Freud pays a lot of attention to something for which I think there is no evidence at all: namely, that Leonardo had a sexless life. All the evidence seems to suggest that he was a homosexual; he was even accused and tried on that account, although acquitted; and during his life was always surrounded by beautiful boys whom he obviously loved. If you read his diaries you will see that he not only loved them but was incredibly patient with them – a point on which Freud touches. There was one nasty little boy, only ten or eleven years old, who was constantly stealing everything he could lay his hands on in Leonardo's studio, yet Leonardo was always bailing him out of trouble, buying him shirts, materials, jackets and suchlike. I believe that Leonardo was probably assumed to be homosexual by his contemporaries, and although homosexuality was then a legal offence, it was not really a social offence to any great extent at all. For example, one of the subsequent famous painters was nicknamed Sodoma because he was a known sodomite.

The emphatic assumption which Freud makes in viewing Leonardo's emotionally impaired sexual life as being related to the scientist-investigator in him and linked to sexual curiosity and the sexual researches of children, is in my opinion unsound. He seems to assume that Leonardo's own statement about the necessity for love to be subsumed under knowledge (a point about which Dr Bion writes) actually means that love *ought* to be subsumed under knowledge, and that one should not love an object until one understands it thoroughly, so that one can then love it for its 'true' qualities. As far as one can see there is no evidence whatsoever to bear out the idea that Leonardo actually lived in this way, or that he was capable of living within the pinched confines of his theory. There is no reason to suppose that during his life as an artist his feuds and intimacies were not as passionate (even if not as noisy) as those of Michelangelo; and certainly the hatred which these two entertained for one another was never doubted by their contemporaries, although Michelangelo was noisy and Leonardo was icy and aloof about it.

Freud makes a very important move here, in that he tries to distinguish between the kind of love which can result from really knowing the true qualities of an object (and loving it for these true qualities), and those conflicting emotions which in fact accompany human relationships. In identifying these last he links them to instinct, by which one assumes he means the feelings that are linked with infantile sexuality: that is to say, love and hate. What he does not distinguish between at this point is curiosity and the thirst for knowledge (that is, the desire to know the truth). Therefore, to refer this to his study of Leonardo, Freud makes no distinction between Leonardo's endless curiosity about everything; which, as is quite clear from his notebooks, included alchemy, witchcraft, necromancy and all sorts of black magic (facts hardly mentioned by Freud); and his genuine thirst for knowledge. For it seems clear that Leonardo was someone whose thirst for knowledge and whose childish curiosity were not differentiated from one another, running hand in hand just as rampantly as his childish preoccupation with toys, all sorts of practical jokes, and startling pyrotechnics ran hand in hand with his most serious scientific investigations and his art work.

The reason Freud felt no necessity for differentiating between Leonardo's childish curiosity and the greatness of his most mature accomplishments (which were always intermingled with one another) is that this differentiation did not exist in Freud's own mind. The result is that his attitude to children's curiosity about sexuality is not at all one that distinguishes a category of hostile intrusiveness on the one hand, from desiring to know and understand the truth on the other. It is at this time that the addendum was made to the *Three Essays* about children's sexuality and the sexual researches of children. But the very fact that he called them 'sexual researches' infuses them with a dignity indicating that he did not make a differentiation between children's destructive and intrusive curiosity and their loving and awestruck desire to understand and know the nature of the world. This is partly due to the fact that Freud saw this curiosity as arising somewhere around the third year; and he therefore tended to link it to either the birth or the expectation of the next baby and thus to his theory that the little boy (the little girl is forgotten), seeing that his little sister docs not have a penis, is mobilized into castration anxiety. This, Freud speculated, drives him first of all to try to find out about the internal world, and secondly, with the onset of latency and its impaired curiosity and desire for knowledge in this area, to abandon finding out. Now I do not think Freud has any evidence for this. He tends to go back to the case of Little Hans, but I think there the evidence is, if anything, that the researches of Little Hans had started long before his third year; and that everything Little Hans was saying about being with his sister in the carriage, and the stork box, contains phantasies that probably long antedate his sister's birth and which are to a certain extent retrospective phantasies. They try, on the basis of later experience, to account for things he observed earlier in his life.

We reach the paper on the Wolf Man; at which point one sees that Freud himself invokes this idea of retrospective curiosity; he construes from the evidence that the Wolf Man made observations at the age of one and a half which he only began to understand retrospectively at the age of four; and that the famous 'wolf ' dream was an attempt to understand something that he had observed at the age of one and a half, possibly at the age of six months, or at the latest two and a half. Thus Freud acknowledges that children make observations at a very early age which continue to puzzle them; and later they make other observations with which they go back to resolve the puzzles that had arisen earlier. According to Freud's theory at this point (1910), we are still to assume that this curiosity is about where babies come from; that it is not in fact aroused until the mother's next pregnancy (or if no pregnancy occurs, the child is still assumed to expect one for some reason that is not given) and that the child is therefore driven primarily by jealousy. It is, according to Freud, the resentment of the birth of this next baby (the expulsion from possession of the mother), and the discoveries about the differences between the sexes (in the case of the little boy having a little sister whose genital he sees and the resultant castration anxiety with its resentment) that cause the curiosity; in other words, it is caused by anxiety and hostility, by jealousy, resentment and the anxiety of castration and of expulsion in favour of the new baby. Since Freud's idea seems to be that this curiosity is fundamentally driven by anxiety and hatred, it is very puzzling that he should think of it as something that should drive the child in the direction of wanting to discover the truth. For his whole theory of repression is based on the assumption that there is a certain necessity or desire to defend *against* knowing the truth (which is also true of his theory of dream formation). And his theory about defence against anxiety entails the defence being made by a distortion of the truth. The theory of repression is mainly a theory of serial distortion of the truth, so that memories are forgotten or else (if they break through the repression) they emerge in a distorted form. Accordingly, the transference is this: the return of the repressed in a distorted form that is not the truth, but is permissible because it has undergone a certain amount of distortion; and it is therefore also equivalent to a dream which is able to enter consciousness for the very reason that it is the truth distorted; and so on. It is very puzzling that children's curiosity should be called 'researches', in the service of the discovery of the truth, when at the same time he is suggesting that it is driven by anxiety and resentment, all the hatred of the Oedipus complex and fear of the birth of a new baby.

When Mrs Klein wrote her first paper in 1921, which was not really an analytic paper but a child observation paper, for some reason, probably through an ignorance of philosophy and perhaps also of Freud's work, she started out without preconceptions about these matters, and observed that a child has a thirst for knowledge which is in the first instance the desire to know all about the mother's body. This thirst for knowledge she thought instinctual in origin but driven by other instincts, first of all by the child's sadism and later by its reparative desires. It is one of the major differences between the work of Mrs Klein and Freud: namely, that a great deal of her work stems from this observation that emotional and intellectual growth are driven by the conflict between love and hate of the mother's body and person. She does say that a certain level of anxiety is necessary for growth and development, but that it is moved by love, and this is the foundation of her concept of the depressive position. The love of the object, and the wish to spare, to serve, to emulate, to give pleasure, is the main driving force in psychic development beyond the more primitive levels.

I draw your attention to this at this point in order to compare it with what is in my opinion the clearest statement in the whole of Freud's writings of his theory of knowledge. His theory of knowledge is not based on a wide philosophical study; he does not write about curiosity or the desire for knowledge with any regard to epistemological theories of the past. It is a purely psychoanalytical theory, to my mind a bad one, which is inconsistent with many of the other facets of his thinking about mental functioning.

In this paper, Freud takes Leonardo to task for his theory of love: that love breaks forth after the full knowing and recognition of the object's true qualities, and is based on this knowledge; and claims that this is not what happens. On the contrary both love and hate are connected with impulses, he says. It is noteworthy that in Freud's work he never does come to a real theory of affects as a central phenomenon in mental functioning; they are seen merely as a by-product of impulse life. At this point he is talking about love and hate and dealing with them as he did in the Rat Man paper, as being at the core of mental conflict. But he does not really think of this conflict as being essentially the loving and the hating in conflict with one another; he is thinking essentially of the impulses, of which the affects are no more than the noise. It is the impulses which are in conflict with one another. So in this respect he has not really come a great distance from his earlier tendency to think of affects as merely manifestations of different levels of excitation in the mental apparatus and therefore fundamentally quantitative rather than qualitative. He has moved a slight distance in recognizing the qualitative distinction between the affects in so far as they relate to different impulses, and are as it were the banners carried by these impulses; each with their different colours, patterns and different kind of noises; but he is not giving them a status of their own nor thinking of the conflict as being essentially emotional conflict. It is still impulse conflict and conflict between the impulse life and the requirements of the outside world. I think it is always important to keep this aspect of Freud's work in mind: that he never came to view anxiety as an affect, but saw it at first as a transformation of impulse, and then later, as a signal and therefore a type of internal information. Even when he passed on to a broader consideration of mental pain, it was tied to the concept of cathexis and thus with excessive accretions of stimuli. This is all relevant to the small section of the first chapter of the Leonardo paper where Freud mentions Leonardo's repression of affects and connects it with his obsessionality and the cold-bloodedness of his investigations: as when he would go to watch men being hanged and tortured in order to study their facial expressions. Furthermore, when he later comes to talk about the expressions on the faces of the Mona Lisa or Saint Anne, Freud discusses them for the purpose of revealing the extent to which Leonardo's emotions were repressed or not available to him, and documents his thesis in a way that is most unconvincing. Take for example the way in which he uses Leonardo's reporting his father's death in his diary with the repetition of 'at seven o'clock' as evidence of emotional repression and of Leonardo not being in contact with his feelings about his father's death. To my mind that is very poor psycho analytic evidence; and is probably more accurately to be taken as demonstrating the way in which the theoretician in Freud can interfere with his respect for the evidence and the data. This part of the paper is nonetheless worthwhile re-reading, because of its instructiveness concerning Freud's idea of love, and its connection with his persistent idea about sublimation. The theory of sublimation is enlarged upon in this paper probably more explicitly than anywhere else.

At this point, however, I wish to turn to the section of the paper dealing with the origin of Leonardo's homosexuality. Freud deals with it as *latent* homosexuality, as homosexual relationships but not homosexual activities. Freud means, as you remember, 'inverted object choice'; and as we see from the *Three Essays,* he does not make any distinction between the man's femininity and the man's homosexuality. Moreover, the concept he produces with regard to Leonardo is one of Leonardo's being narcissistically identified with an androgenous mother, or a rather hermaphrodite figure.

The theory he evokes runs something like this: that Leonardo, an illegitimate child, born to a poor peasant girl, spent the first five years of his life being cuddled and kissed by his mother. There is no evidence at all for this, which is a point to bear in mind although it is irrelevant here since we are talking about Freud's theory of the origins of a particular type of homosexuality. He chose, perhaps quite wrongly, to use Leonardo as if he were a suitable example of it and we should not consider its application to Leonardo himself as serious. What Freud is describing is a little boy without a father, or with a very weak father in his life, who is rather pushed out of the picture by his weakness on the one hand and the mother's androgenous strength and capability on the other; she devotes her entire attention to the little boy and is both gratifying to him and erotically exciting, evoking an intense mutual idealization. At a certain point this little boy begins to have sexual feelings toward his mother; but up to this point it had never occurred to him that she does not have a penis; he is assuming that she does have a penis, and this assumption some-how has the same effect upon him as does the Oedipus complex of another child, and brings about castration anxiety and the repression of his sexuality. And the repression of his sexuality is implemented primarily by means of his identification with the mother, so that his sexuality takes the form of seeking for an object that will be for him the ideal little boy that he was for his mother. It seems to me a good theory; and I am sure that it plays an important part in the genesis of certain types of very motherly homosexuality in men.

I wish to point out that this is the first statement about narcissism: that is, that the person loves a little boy who represents himself, and is therefore loving himself in the boy that he chooses as his sexual object. But it is a theory of narcissism in which is inherent an assumption of an identification; therefore the first theory of narcissism is not just a theory of him loving himself; it is a theory of being identified with the mother and loving himself as does the mother. Later on when we come to the development of Freud's theory of narcissism we will see that it changes; but this is the first statement, and the first statement is of particular importance because it brings out an aspect of narcissism which he tended to neglect later. As we go through the Schreber case and the Wolf Man we will see that the theory of narcissism begins to be filled out phenomenologically, but this idea of identification, which is very central to it, is somewhat lost. However, it is worth noting that at this point, in the first statement of narcissism, 'narcissistic identification' plays a central role. And 36 years later this will develop into Mrs Klein's concept of projective identification as the first description of a mechanism for the accomplishment of a narcissistic identification.

I would like now to say a few words about the ending of the Leonardo paper. I find this very moving; where Freud talks about how he has written a psychoanalytic novel and steps back to take a look at what he has been doing; what he has accomplished and what he has failed to accomplish. What he has to say indicates a very important realization about the nature of psychoanalysis and one which seems to me to have come to him for the first time at this point. Freud undoubtedly had a very strong tendency to think of psychoanalysis as an explanatory science; and all through his work he talks as if it were so. An explanatory science would imply the possibility of prediction, and the idea that psychoanalytic reconstruction would be essentially a demonstration of the inevitability of the person's life-history. I think that this is the only point in Freud's writings where he specifically says that this is not true. There are one or two other places where he talks about chance and fate, but this is the most specific instance in which he states that fate and chance play an overwhelming role in life; and that what psychoanalysis describes is 'what happens'; it does not explain 'why it happens'; and it does not cite the causes of things. So that, had circumstances been different, had the person's constitution been different, had other decisions been made, had other factors entered, the whole life-history could have been different.

CHAPTER EIGHT

The Schreber case (inner world)

I t is of course with a reservation in mind that one includes the Schreber case among Freud's clinical papers, since its content does not relate to experiences in the course of analytical treatment. Freud himself, in a somewhat disingenuous way justifies both its use and the intrusion upon the privacy of the subject, Dr Schreber; but one can see that he was quite enthralled by the *Memoirs* with special reference to the problem which exercised him – perhaps excessively – all through his scientific life: namely that of 'choice of neurosis'. However, it is not from this point of view that I wish to examine the paper, but rather from a more phenomenological one. In a certain sense, Freud was so occupied with using the case as material for exposition that he does not fully explore its rich content. Or at least he does not follow through this exploration. As the prelude to the theory of narcissism it stands close to the Rat Man inapproaching a concept of splitting processes, and it is unique among Freud's writings in approaching a concept of 'the world' as an aspect of mental life.

Schreber's illness, which first manifest itself as a severe hypochondria, metamorphosed during its second phase into a paranoid deterioration, the chief persecutor of which was his previous physician, and then slowly underwent an elaboration into a grandiose delusional system in which the figure of God played a highly ambiguous role: half persecutor, half lover. It is characteristic of Freud's boldness that he could take an interest in these highly bizarre phenomena on the basis of an assumption that they were, nonetheless, comprehensible derivatives of the common impulses of the human mind. But while it is a bold stand, it may also be accused of a certain pedestrian determination which emerges at times, even to Freud's embarrassment, as when he has to apologise to the reader for the interpretation that the sun, whose rays Schreber boasts of being able to look upon with his naked eyes, is in the last analysis a symbol for the father. This reductionism is, of course, typical of Freud and one may cite this case as the most cogent example of the way in which his theory of symbolism tends to take the life out of things. Thus the defence for examining the *Memoirs* as derivative, of common human impulses neglects the opposite possibility, namely that just such complex constructions may always, in some less disordered way, underlie the phenomenology of mental health. For instance, Freud consistently refers to Schreber's delusion of being transformed into a woman as a process of 'emasculation' but it is quite clear that in Schreber's mind the removal of his masculine attributes was a simple process compared with the complexity of endowing him with femininity. This represents then the same limited view that infuses all of Freud's views on sexuality: castration complex, children's sexual researches, etc. It can be traced to the preconception that femininity is essentially passive and derivative, a view quite in keeping with the history of Hellenic, Judaic and Christian thought. For instance it is of interest to note how similar in many ways is Schreber's cosmology and anatomy to that of Plato, as described in the *Timaeus*, in which the congruence between man and God is described in detail. The chief difference is perhaps that in his ambivalence to God, Schreber attributes to him the defect that he docs not understand living creatures but only dead ones. His assumption that the 'basic language of God' is an antiquated German is not different from the Judaeo-Christian one that Hebrew was the universal language before God punished the people of Babylon for their presumptuous tower by inflicting the confusion of tongues, which Jesus then rectified for his apostles by his 'gift of tongues'. Our modern counterpart is perhaps Chomsky's universal generative grammar.

Thus it is that Schreber's relations to God and the sun may be viewed not as a boring elaboration of a child's relation to its father but as indeed a fascinating description, marred by intense ambivalence, of an elaborate unconscious phantasy, with its multiple splitting, variety of qualities and attributes, and diversity of functions, which underlies the conscious, simplistic conception. One need only take into account the reversal, by which God becomes childish and Schreber emerges victorious from their struggle, to see the normal child's conflict. But this reversal, with its attendant confusions, is not quite correctly seen by Freud with respect to the question of voluptuousness, for it is quite clear that Schreber has equated the voluptuousness of defaecation with that of the feminine experience in coitus. Correspondingly his sexual relation to God is that of a concubine, not a wife, as Freud insists. Amusingly, the subject of confusion of zones and functions only emerges as a joke about futility of interpretation: 'holding a sieve under a he-goat while someone else milks it'. One must consider that Freud had no conceptual framework as yet for differentiating between feminine and homosexual in Schreber's case, although he could easily see that contempt for women (the miracle birds, emphasis on the buttocks as the genital area, attribution of preoccupation with voluptuousness) was essential. This lack of differentiation mars the value of the important conclusion Freud was so keen to put forward: namely the connection between paranoia and passive homosexuality. Consequently the 'simple formula' by which love is turned into hate takes on a rather gimmicky quality. The concept of 'homosexual libido' has to be linked to castration anxiety and Adler's 'masculine protest' in order to explain the anxiety and revulsion it arouses. Because of this Freud's investigation of the means by which the 'reconciliation' between the paranoid and the grandiose delusional illnesses was brought about, loses much of its force.

But this brings us to the most fascinating and brilliant part of the paper, the 'world destruction' phantasy and Freud's investigation of its nature and consequences. Having noted the similarity between the structure of Flechsig and God in the two periods of the illness, Freud concluded that the development of the paranoia was related to a process of 'decomposition, or, more precisely, that 'paranoia resolves once more into their elements the products of the condensations and identifications which are effected in the unconscious' (i.e. in the course of development, I take it). This 'decomposition' is first investigated from the point of view of regression of the libido to the stage of narcissism as a development mid point between autoerotism and object-love – a view he had already put forward in the 1910 edition of the *Three Essays on Sexuality*. The defensive process against this regression is seen as aimed at the renewed 'sexualisation of the social instincts'. The 'simple formula' for turning love into hate is produced here and elaborated later in the paper on 'Jealousy, paranoia and homosexuality' (1922). To this formula he needed only add the concept of projection as an externalisation of an internal perception, to derive a satisfying explanation of paranoia. And here we find his most detailed account of the relation of fixation, repression and eruption; or the 'return of the repressed'. It is in relation to this last that Freud discusses the 'world destruction' phantasy. (Here I believe there is an important error in translation: p. 68 reads 'and during the last part of his stay in Flechsig's clinic he believed that the catastrophe had already occurred and he was the only real man alive.' It should read: 'and at the climax of his illness he believed that the catastrophe had occurred during the last part of his stay.' Freud writes that 'the end of the world is the "projection of his internal catastrophe"' but hedges about its mechanism. In the text he attributes it to Schreber's 'withdrawal of his love' from his 'subjective world' but in a footnote, where he quotes a poem from Goethe's *Faust*, it is attributed to the work of a 'powerful fist'. It is the rebuilding of this shattered 'subjective world' that is the work of the delusion formation. 'The paranoiac builds it again, not more splendid, it is true, but at least so that he can once more live in it.'

This brilliant analysis of the mechanisms by which the transition from the early paranoid to the later grandiose delusion is effected is, I think, the farthest point of advance in Freud's conceptualising of the mental apparatus and adumbrates the work on cyclothymia in *Mourning and Melancholia*, while providing the jumping-off place for Abraham's last work and the developments of Melanie Klein. One must go back to the statement that 'paranoia resolves once more into their elements the products of the condensations and identifications that are effected in the unconscious' to see that Freud held some theory of how the 'subjective world' is constructed in the course of development.

Thus we can see that the wonderful step forward, from the clinical point of view, represented by the Schreber case, is that of the conceptualisation of the inner world: the formulation of projection as a mechanism, and the introduction into the concept of narcissism of a new concreteness related to 'condensations and identifications'; it is, nonetheless, somewhat attenuated by the restrictions imposed by the Libido Theory. The new theory proposed in 1920 in 'Beyond the pleasure principle' freed him from this restriction and enabled a new, more complicated approach to the comprehension of the perversions, by way of the phenomenon of masochism and its relation to destructive impulses. Here in the Schreber case he is hard pressed to account for the fact that the world destruction phantasy came *between* the delusions of persecution and the grandiose system. He falls back on the idea of a partial detachment of the libido and gets into something of a muddle in relation to 'ego-cathexes' and 'cathexes of the ego'. In the hedging about the 'fist' smashing the world to bits in paranoid fury, we can see Freud's chief difficulty and link it to his lack of conceptual equipment of a concrete inner or 'subjective' world that could be so smashed. Shaken by these difficulties, Freud ends his attempt at formulation with wryly noting the striking similarity between Schreber's delusions and Freud's theories in so far as the one lays so much emphasis on the 'rays of God' and the other on 'distribution of the libido'. 'It remains for the future to decide whether there is more delusion in my theory than I should like to admit or whether there is more truth to Schreber's delusion than other people are as yet prepared to believe.'

CHAPTER NINE

Mourning and melancholia (identification processes)

I would like to discuss now that rather interesting period in the early years of the First World War when Freud had very few patients, since his students were mainly from abroad, and when he had time to think and take stock of the science which he had fathered – or mothered. He realized that there were great difficulties in every direction: in the training direction, in the theoretical direction, in the technical direction and also in conceiving its place in the world and what it might reasonably mean as part of the culture. He had been considerably stirred up earlier by the so-called defections of Adler and Jung and in the years from 1910 or 1911 onward there are outbursts against them in his writings every once in a while. They are interesting outbursts because their content often suggests that he is reviling them for just those things about which he is really troubled himself and with which he has not yet come to grips. For example, much of what he reviles Jung for will in fact later turn into his revision of instinct theory, although it is of course not quite the same as Jung's theory. He is reviling Jung for abandoning the central role of sexuality, the libido theory and so on in favour of something that he considered to be a watered-down, popularly acceptable product. Twelve or fifteen years later, it changes in his own hands into the new instinct theory, in which sexuality is not given this primary place but has to take its position within the life instincts and be opposed to what he calls the 'death instinct'. Similarly in his reviling of Adler, mainly for his masculine protest and his will-to-power theories, one finds the harbingers of Freud's later struggle with the whole problem of hatred and evil and destructiveness, which finally became the concept of the death instinct.

Therefore, even though it is rather annoying to see him stop and beat these fellows every once in a while as one goes through his writings, it is interesting to study the content of his irritation, which reveals something about his character. When he was at his most positive and authoritative – even authoritarian – he was often on the verge of having the greatest doubts and misgivings and throwing himself into the problem of revising his own thinking. A considerable amount of this sort of beating goes on in the period from 1911 to 1913, and then begins a whole series of 're-thinking' papers. I do not want to spend much time on the re-thinking and re-formulating papers and I am not going to discuss the technical papers, though these are interesting because one can see that when faced with the problem of training people to practise analysis he really had to think about his own technique. This brought him up against the problem I have been highlighting throughout these chapters: namely, the split between what he did and what he said or thought he did. In these technical papers he resolves this split quite substantially. There are papers on transference love and starting analysis, dream analysis, the new concept of 'working through'. These are important because they represent his realization that (as he said) just presenting the solution is not the end of the analyst's task. You remember that he earlier scolded Elizabeth and Dora because they did not accept his solution (and the dream of Irma's injection revolves around this problem). Now, however, he reaches the conclusion that these intellectual solutions in themselves do not constitute the analytical method; but that the whole economic task of enabling the patient to accept and to make use of these insights for bringing the unconscious into consciousness (as he was then thinking about it) is also the task of the analyst. One can not just throw the patient out once the jigsaw puzzle has been solved to the analyst's amusement or satisfaction. Therefore these technical papers are very interesting.

And then there is the series of 'metapsychological papers'. Not until this time did Freud decide that he was founding a quite new branch of psychology, which had to be distinguished from other psychologies because it was based on different kinds of data and method. Also, it was characterised by its concern with four different categories of mental functioning, which at that time he was calling: the topographic (or different levels of consciousness); the dynamics (mechanisms of mental functioning); the genetic or developmental; and the economic. So, although they are fairly theoretical, these papers are also of technical interest, particularly the paper on repression. And I would like to try to extract the changing view of the world and of life that is hidden and embodied in his theories of this time, when by virtue of coming to a conviction about the importance of the phenomenology of narcissism, Freud was just on the verge of a complete remodelling of his conception of the mind. The change from the so-called topographic model to what we now call the structural conception of ego, id and superego, was brewing.

It seems to have been the phenomenology of narcissism that most impressed and moved him; and the paper on narcissism is an attempt to gather together what he had already been saying for four – or perhaps five – years. Part of it had been stated in the analysis of the Schreber memoirs, yet more in the Leonardo paper, and now in this paper he draws it together with some of the ordinary life phenomena – as in his discussion of falling ill, falling in love and hypochondria. From them he abstracts a conception of the development of the capacity for instincts to seek objects starting with a period of primary narcissism (later 'auto-erotism'), in which identification with objects is almost indistinguishable from the choice of an object (in the first instance the body of the person himself).

In reading this paper one sees some very interesting aspects of the change in Freud's conception of the world. He is uneasy about his previous ambition, so much of which was previewed in the *Project* of 1897. He is struggling still (as later in the paper on *Mourning and Melancholia*) with the whole question of mental pain and is still inclined to think of it as un-pleasure and in terms of excitation. In one place he even calls it 'painful unpleasure' – by which time he is at least acknowledging that it really hurts, and that it plays an important part in the processes of the mind. However, the whole issue of mental pain is thrown into a state of disorder in his mind by his coming at this time upon the tricky and difficult problem of identification: that is, the problem of 'whose pain is it really?' It is from this angle that he discusses the question of being in love and particularly the question of hypochondria, which I think Freud handles with very canny intelligence, recognizing that it involves the problem of 'who is ill?' and 'who is suffering?' There is present in hypochondria the same phenomenon that he is going to discuss later in *Mourning and Melancholia.* In the relation of mania and melancholia he saw a certain commerce in mental pain: that is, necessitating the questions 'who is having the pleasure?', and 'what really happens to the pain?' Owing to the fact that he is becoming aware that pain is something that can be distributed – that the person in whom it originates is not merely stuck with it, but can get rid of it in some way – he is also aware that the neuroses which he has been studying all these years are not just problems of a person defending himself against having mental pain or unacceptable ideas or repellent memories, but in so far as there is a problem about mental pain there is also a problem about its distribution. For although there are means (mainly by the mechanism of repression) of remaining unaware of the pain that is going on in oneself, there are also other methods of getting rid of it into various objects in the outside world; there is a certain transportation of mental pain, not simply defence against it. Its location can be shifted, rather than its existence denied.

If we return to the Rat Man and the clinical notes on the case, we will see that Freud was acutely aware that this played an important part in the transference: that the transference had not simply an ideational content (that is, phantasies that were transferred on to the analyst), but that it also involved a commerce in mental pain. In those notes it is apparent that Freud was aware that his patient was causing him distress. When he describes in his discussion of obsessional neurosis what he calls the 'isolating of the affects' (separating the affects from the phantasy and ideational content) he was quite aware that these affects were going somewhere, particularly in so far as they were painful. The patient was imposing on Freud very painful affects; humiliating him, angering him by degrading his love objects: his wife, his daughters and so on. He was acutely aware that his carrying the transference was not simply a matter of his being the object of the patient's erotic desires or castration anxiety. One can but admire his impressive patience and good humour. So it seems to me that by this time, Freud at work was much more aware that his business was with the economics of mental pain and that pain is not merely absence of pleasure and the result of too much or too little stimulation in the psychic apparatus.

I have already suggested how Freud became aware, particularly in the Schreber case, of the need to conceptualise a person's world; and that this became necessary because he saw how the world was either falling to pieces or being knocked to pieces for Schreber. We have Freud's brilliant realisation that it was this rebuilding, in a very bizarre way, of the 'subjective' inner world that had fallen to pieces, that created the noisy delusional part of the illness, the attempt at recovery. I suggested that in the earlier paper on Leonardo he had become aware of the necessity for trying to conceive of a person's life as a continuity and an entity; it was not possible as he had thought initially just to tease out little memories and little theories of events, and link them to symptoms; this was not a task commensurate with the stature of psychoanalytic thought and the expectations and hopes of those people who were attracted to it. Psychoanalysis had to become a discipline which undertook to try to understand and construct theories about all the evidence which it elicited. Consequently Freud became preoccupied not only with symptoms but with character. We have the paper on 'Character and anal erotism'; then a few years later a lovely paper called 'Character types met with in analysis', in which he gives a round description of character types which we all know very well, having been all three of them ourselves at different times: one describes 'the exceptions', who think that what applies to other people does not apply to them because they are special; another, 'criminals from a sense of guilt'; and the third, 'people who are wrecked by success'. The people described here are all familiar: people in whose characters these different facets are such dominating and persistent features that their whole lives become coloured by them – whereas you and I only suffer from them every few minutes.

So one sees that Freud's interest was extending at this period: not only to character, but to anthropology, to the history of comparative religion, to the problem of art and creativity, to civilization as a process about which his 19th-century optimism was waning. His interest in life and his wish to apply psychoanalysis to everything that came within his ken at this time is quite clear. Moreover, one receives the impression that the phenomenology of narcissism as he had met with it in the Schreber case and in his attempts to understand homosexuality on the one hand, and creativity on the other, in Leonardo; combined with the narcissistic phenomena that he had come upon in relation to such things as falling in love, hypochondria and people's behavior during physical illness, moved him towards thinking of the mind in a much more organized way. It is only around 1915 that the view with which we are now so familiar, of the libido developing in progressive stages of organization (instead of there merely being trends in infantile sexuality) emerged as part of his thinking. The step of beginning to think of the mind in an organized and not merely in an operational way, was leading Freud to dissatisfaction with the topographic theory with its overwhelming preoccupation with levels of consciousness and its psychopathology. This was too narrow a framework.

Now I would like to turn our particular attention to the rather marvellous paper on *Mourning and Melancholia* and, through both this and the paper 'On narcissism', to focus upon three problems with which Freud tried to grapple. The most important of these, as already mentioned, and one which actually gave him trouble in his clinical work, is the problem of identification; secondly, the concept of the ego-ideal is beginning to develop and will become later the concept of the superego; and there is, finally, the attempt to come more firmly to grips with the problem of mental pain.

Even before the Schreber case, in a sporadic way, it is clear that Freud felt the necessity of accounting for people's sense of being observed and watched. In a way, it is a remarkable thing that no inkling of the idea of conscience enters into his work for the first twenty years. It is only now, in 1919, under the pressure of these clinical phenomena, of people feeling them selves to be scrutinized, watched over and criticized in a rather paranoid way, that he feels the need to bring together two concepts which have been rather held apart in his thinking to date. He had produced the theory of the dream censor; then there was something called castration anxiety (which some un specified figure of phantasy was mobilizing). Now he singles out these phenomena of feeling observed and scrutinized. But he is also aware of yet another phenomenon which needs to be accounted for and linked closely with the above, one that has to do with quite the opposite: namely, feeling encouraged and supported. His first attempt to deal with this is in the concept of the ideal ego. This is quite different from the ego-ideal; the ideal ego is connected with a conception of the golden times of the past, of the time when His Majesty the baby was courted and enjoyed the megalomania, the narcissism and the omnipotence that is, as it were, the right of every baby. The conception of this idealized self, and the wish to recover that state of bliss and universal admiration, is formulated as the concept of the ideal ego. And from this, by reversing the idea, comes the concept of the ego-ideal. It stands outside the ego or self and keeps pointing to the ideal ego, saying, 'You used to be like that, so blissful, and you can become like that again.' Thus the ego-ideal is a rather gentle and encouraging figure, and Freud somehow manipulates the concept of narcissism so that the relation between the self and the ego-ideal begins to be something like a love relationship. Indeed, it is something very similar to what he describes in Leonardo's relationship to his boys, in which the artist is seen to be identified with his mother, loving and idealizing him as a little boy. Freud begins to think that this is within the realm of narcissism; that the ego and the ego-ideal (with the conception of the ideal ego in mind, as it were) can enter into a sort of blissful love relationship which, since it has to do with states of bliss or elation, is part of the phenomenology of narcissism. And he is thinking, perhaps, that this may be the core or substance of happiness.

This bears an important relation to his general idea of love at this time: because nowhere in his conceptions of it does loving develop beyond this seeking for gratification. And although he talks about loving, in libido terms, as the object being invested not only with the object libido but also with the ego libido, so that the ego becomes depleted and impoverished in favour of the object, yet to his mind this is always done with the aim of getting it back again. The move is thus a sort of capital investment aimed at obtaining a profit; you cannot exactly think of yourself as a benefactor of mankind when, by loving, you set up a factory, as it were, rather than endowing a charity. Freud's attachment to the libido theory, which must seek to explain things simply on the basis of the distribution of libido, binds him to the idea that mental pain is radically connected to maldistribution of the libido; that the absence of pleasure derives from either a dammed-up libido or – as he is thinking at this stage – from a drained-out and impoverished libido. And it is precisely because he is bound to this energetics theory that it is not possible for him to construct within its framework a conception of love that goes beyond enlightened self-interest. It remains really for Mrs Klein's formulation of the depressive position to carry psycho-analysis over that hump. Now Freud keeps within this concep-tion of an observing agency: one that stands outside the self criticizing or, as he was still thinking of it, encouraging; and he sees that it has some thing to do with identification processes. He actually calls them narcissistic identifications by this stage; and proceeds in the paper on *Mourning and Melancholia* to the quite brilliant dissection of these four stages of mind: the melan-cholic state and its relation to the mourning state; the manic state and its relation to bliss, ecstasy and triumph over adversity. The discovery he seems to make – and one which I find most compelling myself – is as follows: though the melancholic and the person in mourning are strikingly similar in appearance, on careful examination one finds first of all that they are not in pain in the same way; that the pain of the melancholic has something to do with a depletion of himself, whereas that of the person in mourning arises because, owing to the loss of his love object from the world, the world has become empty. It would seem that the melancholic depletes himself through somehow becoming identified and completely mixed up with an object that is not experienced plainly as lost, but as depleted, denigrated, reviled and accused.

At this point in the differentiation it seems that Freud him self becomes very mixed-up, being unsure whether it is the ego accusing or, the ego-ideal turning against the ego. However, the relevant point is that he has come to realize that there is a question: 'Who is in pain?' – is it the ego or its object that is in pain; and 'Who is the one that is being reviled?' – is the person truly reviling himself or is he reviling the part of him self that is identified with an object that, at another level, he is really accusing. Freud comes to realize that while mourning states are terminable by virtue of the very painful process of relinquishment of all the memories, hopes, expectations related to the love object in the outside world, melancholia can terminate only when the object has been actually ground into the dust and is either dead or so completely denigrated that the ego can triumph over it. It is for this reason that melancholia tends to slip over into mania; and the mania is essentially a triumph over and a liberation from an object that was originally so superior that it commanded love, and then was disappointing or hurtful in a way that aroused terrible rage and hatred. Then through this process of attacking it while at the same time identifying with it, the destructive process is carried to completion. It was only a few years later that Abraham was able to describe how the completion of this process was a bodily act as well as a mental state; where defaecating out of the body an object that had now been turned to faeces was representative of defaecating out of the mind as well, and triumphing over it in its reduction to absolute rubbish. Abraham was then able to discover the next step in our understanding of melancholia, which Freud was not in a position to recognize: namely, that the identification with the object that Freud had described in melancholia recurs and the mania relapses into melancholia because this defaecated-out object is compulsively re-introjected (coprophagic phantasy). This has something to do with the way in which the destroyed object gets back inside and the way in which it becomes identified with once again, causing the mania to collapse into melancholia once more. Thus one sees a basis for a circular process in the cyclothymias.

The core of these discoveries is the realization that mental pain is the central problem and, quite apart from satisfaction or frustration of the libido, an article of commerce between the ego and its object; for once this is recognized one can no longer presume that the person who seems to be in pain is in fact in pain himself, but one must consider that he may be manifesting this mysterious process of identification with an object in pain. Of course Freud knew that identification could play a role in hysterical phenomena. You will recall that he was thinking of hysteria as being just a little thread of memory running through the personality, with a symptom on the end and a traumatic experience at the beginning. He had now to think of hysteria as a way of life and of an hysterical person, which meant a revision in his whole framework. It is interesting to observe that in certain of his writings of this period – such as the essays on war and those containing sociological and anthropological thought – Freud seems to be weighed down by an absolutely appalling and pessimistic view of the world. And while this was naturally a facet of everybody's reaction to the war, one must remember that Freud was seeing it fairly exclusively from the point of view of psychoanalysis at the stage it had then reached. That is to say, he was thinking that the difficulty with deformations of character originated in the repression of instincts and damming-up of the libido; and that from this ensued either anxiety – still seen as the consequence and not the cause of repression – or, in so far as the instincts were being frustrated and deprived of expression, soured love in the form of hatred. I would like once more to stress this conception of love as being the desire to gratify these erotic instincts at whatever level they happen to be: auto-erotic, narcissistic or object-related, at whatever erogenous zone; and as a desire which, when frustrated, metamorphoses through ambivalence to hatred. For its immediate corollary is the naive and, indeed, presently popular, theory that all the trouble in the world is owing to people not enjoying themselves; that it is not evil in the world nor anything vicious, violent and destructive in human nature that makes us rather beastly to one another, but simply the unaccountable absence of a blissful happiness.

The abdication from responsibility inherent in this idea, combined with the then current history of war, naturally eliminated any possibility that the world should seem to be getting better; it could only seem, of necessity, to be deteriorating. Indeed, in Freud's writing that primitive tribes did not suffer from this suppression which produces repression which in turn imposes restrictions upon their gratification – a theory quite incompatible with his talking about cannibalism – one is witnessing precisely this pessimism expressed in anthropological terms. His idea of 'primitive', in spite of his anti-religiosity, begins to sound like the Garden of Eden. One is led to imagine that it is as if things have been getting worse and worse since Adam and Eve were chased out of the Garden, or since the most primitive tribes began to be civilized and impose the necessity of making a living upon their children. I do not suggest for a moment that these are Freud's precise terms of argument, but wish to illustrate how the undervaluation of pain was costing him any hope about the possibility of health or happiness. He only found relief from this pessimism in his very last years when he began to formulate the question rather more properly to himself and to allow better for the terrific complexity of the personality structure. For the three-part structure that he begins to discern now and finally describes in 'The ego and the id' is in fact far more complicated than the earlier idea of an ego with instincts that it somehow had to manage in the face of an outside world which it had simultaneously to satisfy. Clearly this development with the discovery, inevitable to it, of the splitting processes and the understanding that health and illness can exist side by side in the same personality, allows for a more optimistic view. However, I think one has to realize that a truly optimistic conception would have to be one that thought of love as something beyond enlightened self-interest; and in order to get beyond this conception of love, Freud was going to have to discard this energetics theory and the idea of un-pleasure, and really come to grips with a more purely psychological theory, in which 'pain' really was what it meant: that is, it really hurts and is not just the absence of something pleasant.

CHAPTER TEN

The Wolf Man (the primal scene)

The case of the 'Wolf Man' is to my mind the most important case history in the whole of psychoanalytic literature and in all of Freud's work; for the Wolf Man was what might be called an encyclopaedia of psychopathology. Moreover, I believe this particular case was Freud's premier clinical experience because all the work that follows seems to be deeply involved with it. It opened up the phenomenon of the primal scene to him. Now this was something which Freud had in fact conceptualized very early on, but which – probably owing to his diminished interest in the idea of specific aetiology – he later put aside. It was not until he was faced with the Wolf Man and his extraordinary dream and the evidence of the impact of the dream on the child's development, that Freud took it up again. In a way it is this theory that gives proper psychoanalytic form to all of Freud's theories about sexuality; for although they had been, as it were, announced in the *Three Essays on Sexuality*, they were not built upon a foundation of psychoanalytic data, but merely from psychoanalytical modes of thought applied to ordinary medical and psychiatric data.

In the case of the Wolf Man, however, the data and reconstruction are purely psychoanalytical; and for that very reason it is convincing only in so far as one is already convinced. In other words, for people who view psychoanalysis from the outside it stands as a particularly ridiculous episode in psychoanalytic literature. From the evidence of a dream remembered from childhood, Freud reconstructs a scene of parents in their underclothes during the day, having intercourse three times from behind, witnessed by a child of one and a half years, who passed a stool. One can understand that it might seem ridiculous, but it is probably quite correct and, in the context of Ruth Mack Brunswick's account fifteen years later of her subsequent treatment of the Wolf Man, the dream is most enlightening. For during this second analysis – which was only of six months' duration – the Wolf Man produced the most marvellous sequence of dreams in the midst of a paranoid breakdown from which she helped him to recover; and these dreams are almost all concerned with the original wolf dream and its significance in his life. In point of fact, this writing is more 'convincing' than anything Freud wrote; furthermore a large body of subsequent literature has grown up about the Wolf Man: Muriel Gardner's account of his life after the treatment with Ruth Mack Brunswick and his life experiences during the Second World War; his own book – which came out in 1973 – about his analysis with Freud. It is an immensely well-documented case history and is, as I have said before, the premier case history of psychoanalysis.

The sudden development in Freud's thinking at this time was certainly influenced by this case. It started in 1910 and finished in 1914, interrupted by the First World War when the Wolf Man went back to his native Russia. There the revolution of 1917 swept away his fortune; he turned up impoverished and a little ill in Vienna and saw Freud for a few months in 1918 or 1919. It is worth noting that Freud collected money for his financial support for years in Vienna; for it was precisely this collecting of money that elicited from the Wolf Man a kind of parasitism of Freud and the psychoanalytic movement, and really precipitated his breakdown and the character traits associated with it in 1926.

It is therefore a case which throws a revealing light on Freud's character and on his relationship to his patients. For on the one hand Freud must have established this charity because he felt that this man's case history had made such a contribution to psychoanalysis that he deserved a kind of honorarium from the movement; and to my mind, this attitude, with its implicit understanding that psychoanalysis is the work of both patient and analyst, is fundamentally a correct one. Nevertheless on the other hand, I believe Freud in fact felt somewhat guilty towards this patient, largely as a result of the manoeuvre that he utilized for what might be called stampeding him into action. For with some three and a half to four years of desultory work behind him, and nothing to show for it but a continuing punctilious co-operation and utter absence of any feeling or involvement in the transference relationship, Freud became quite discouraged and set an irrevocable termination date. In the next six or nine months the most convincing reconstructive material was collected. As Freud indicated in a footnote in the case history, it was a tactic that he subsequently regretted.

However, in addition to the regret regarding technical procedure, I suspect there was another area of his work for this man about which he had misgivings; and about which the Wolf Man held a grievance that was to come out very strongly in his work with Ruth Mack Brunswick. For the prolonged illness had started out as a breakdown of a very hypochondriacal nature, during which he was terribly paranoid towards various people who carried the name 'Wolf': his dentist, his doctor; and indeed he was extremely paranoid towards Freud and, at one stage, probably quite dangerous to him. Now Freud was already ill with cancer of the jaw – a fact which must have weighed heavily in his decision not to take the treatment upon himself, and which also played some part in the hypochondriacal aspect of the Wolf Man's breakdown, as he had some inkling of it. However, his murderousness toward Freud was not based solely on an unresolved aspect of the transference; it was also related to the way in which Freud seems to have pushed the theory of sublimation very hard with this man, and urged him to sublimate his homosexuality by studying law and jurisprudence. This was quite contrary to the man's wishes and interests and he seems to have felt very coerced about it by Freud. Indeed I think there is probably much truth in the idea that Freud was still so utterly convinced by his theory that sublimated homosexuality was the source of the greatest cultural achievements, that he pushed for sublimation once he felt that he had satisfactorily analysed the infantile foundations of the homosexuality.

It is in this area, to my mind, that there was an exception in the technique used by Freud which was otherwise, by this time, purely analytical. That is to say, in the area of sublimation this concept was linked to the Libido Theory with its idea of there being a uniform mental energy dammed-up by repressions. At best, this energy could be prevented from release into a free flow that would emerge as infantile perversions and polymorphous sexuality, and could be channelled into sublimations to emerge as socially useful types of behaviour. Freud was almost totally convinced by this, basically owing to his commitment to the libido theory at that time. While this clinical work was going on – between 1910 and 1914 – Freud was just in the process of realizing the area of narcissism and the phenomenology connected with it, and he was altering his instincts theory, but only to distinguish more between object libido and narcissistic libido, rather than between sexual instincts and life-preservative instincts; however, this did not really amount to an important shift in his thinking.

Finally, and before we come to concentrate our attention on the problem of the primal scene, I would like to mention other aspects which clarify its setting in Freud's mind. The most important issue is that of the dream. As I mentioned earlier, Freud placed dreaming in a rather trivial position in people's lives, assigning to it this rather unimportant quasi-physiological function of helping the dreamer to stay asleep by providing him with hallucinatory gratifications of his unconscious infantile wishes. However, in his clinical work, Freud never behaved according to this belief: take, for example, the emphasis on the repetitiveness of Dora's dreams; the attention paid to the Rat Man's dreams and their role in the elucidation of the transference, and the way in which the Rat Man's reaction to his dreams is taken as having important emotional reality for him. And when we arrive at this present paper, Freud is dealing with a dream of a child of about four years of age to which he attributes an absolutely crucial role in the child's whole development.

It is in fact somewhat puzzling to see just how Freud saw this dream as functioning, when one remembers that he considered it to be such a crucial event. Naturally, he is at first uncertain in his own mind and leaves quite open the question of the dating of the primal scene, to which the dream is supposed to be a reference and from which the primal scene is reconstructed. He thinks it is at one and a half but it could have been at six months, it could have been at two and a half: he derives, half-jokingly I think, the formula of $n + 6$ months. However, it seems to me that he hedges an important problem: namely, whether it was the primal scene itself that had the impact on the child, or whether it was the dream that he had between one and a half and three and a half years later which gave retrospective significance and impact to the primal scene. And owing to this indecision as to scene and dream, he also has to leave undecided whether we are dealing with a scene or with a phantasy. In this particular instance he seems fairly convinced that what he has reconstructed is a scene; but of course he leaves open the question as to whether it was the scene or the dream that had the impact or that organized the experience in retrospect. Then – from the point of view of developing the theory of psychosexual development, in which we are going to place a primal something – he has to leave open the question as to whether we are going to talk about a primal scene, or a primal phantasy. Thus, are we going to think of it as something constitutional, hereditary, a preconception carried with us from the primordal history of the race, etc.; or as something quite inevitable in the life of every child? To take the latter case, naturally we would have to deal with children who do not have both parents or are raised in hostels with a changing nursing staff and so on; but, needless to say, he does not have any data about these situations at this point.

There is some evidence for the first viewpoint. Let us take, for instance, the children of Anna Freud's 'Bulldog Bank' study, who were perhaps born in the concentration camp, passed around and in some mysterious way kept alive; having had nothing like parental care in any continuous way from their actual parents, they were then brought together in this home in Bulldog Bank, where it was found that as their primary defensive grouping broke up and they began to develop, they began to show ordinary oedipal manifestations. Such evidence does very strongly suggest that not only is the Oedipus complex part of our constitutional predisposition and universally present, but that the expectation of the primal scene is so absolutely built into the apparatus of mental life that we consider it to be an ubiquitous phantasy. Being pressing, in any life situation where there are two parents in a child's life, it eventually produces for him a primal scene, even if it is not seen but heard, smelled or whatever: that is, an experience of being alone in the atmosphere of a parental intercourse going on somewhere.

Freud seems to think that the impact of actually viewing the parents in intercourse is probably greater and more likely to be traumatic than bearing or any other source of evidence from which the child construes that it is going on at that moment, and which lights up his predisposition to this particular phantasy. I would say from my own experience that I do not see any compelling evidence that the viewing is more important in itself than, say, the hearing – which is what we find evidence of in the middle-class people with whom we are accustomed to deal. What we find evidence of nowadays is that where a child has been exposed to the viewing of a primal scene, he has, in our culture and the class of our culture with which we generally deal, been exposed also to a particular type of psychopathology in the parents who wish to expose their intercourse to the child, and behave therefore not with a special insensitivity but with a special inclination and determination to involve the child in the visual experience of the intercourse. So with the kind of patients whom we treat, when we find evidence of actual viewing, we expect to find evidence of parental psychopathology and not just fortuitous occurrence. Of course there are cases of the child toddling in in the middle of the night and so on, but even that is not the sort of thing that turns up in our material today.

In Freud's time however, things were really quite different: children probably always slept in their parents' bedroom for the first few years of their lives or until the next baby came along, or else slept in a room with servants, in wealthier families, and were exposed to their sexual activities. For Freud to reconstruct from his clinical material a primal scene as a visual experience in the middle of the day, is a far less unlikely event and far less likely to imply parental pathology than it would in our day. Therefore the reconstruction did not surprise Freud as a social phenomenon;

what surprised him was the evidence of the immense impact on the child.

I think it is important to realize that at this time Freud's ideas on development were becoming much more complicated and more organized; he was not only thinking in terms of the 'vicissitudes of instinct' as he calls it, the development of erogenous zones from oral to anal to phallic to genital; he was thinking also in terms of the total characterological development of the child and of the individual. Although one has to say that Freud was not interested in children a few years later (directly: in their development as a phenomenon in itself; whereas he was mainly interested in reconstructing the childhood background of his adult patients' pathology), yet nonetheless he was at this time beginning to see the development of children in a much more unified form, and as something of great complexity. In the Leonardo paper we saw him trying to conceptualize a person as having a whole life which needs to be understood as an entity; in the Schreber case he was approaching the concept of a person who has to live in both the outside world and in his 'subjective' world which he can pull to pieces, or at least pull out something which holds it together so that it falls to pieces. Then there came the papers on character development, on anal character; and a few years later the papers on three interesting character types. Thus his whole view of mental life was really beginning to cohere and to cause him to conceive more fully of a person with a development which takes place in a particular milieu. Where in the cases of the Rat Man and Dora, one hears little or nothing of the mother, here in the Wolf Man case for instance, not only is she imminent in his adult life as someone who handles the money (she gives him a meagre allowance which causes them to row every once in a while like an unhappily married couple), but also one hears about the impact of his mother's personality on him as a child: how she tried to deal with his naughtiness by taking him to see the religious pictures, and how she succeeded in inculcating religion, which instituted his obsessional period. We hear about the impact of her menorrhagia and her gynaecological troubles, her saying to the doctor that she 'could not go on living like that', the family moving from one house to another, from the summer place to the winter place; the intricacies of the Wolf Man's relation to servants; the impact of his sister's character, how she seduced him sexually and tyrannized over him with her cleverness, and her very forceful and pathological character; and his reaction to her later committing suicide – the background all unfolds. One gets a much more complete, Tolstoyan picture of a whole community and people growing up in it, of a life being led amidst other lives. It absolutely springs to life. And just as Freud said his *Studies on Hysteria* read like short stories, so does this read something like a novel, and leaves one with the same sense of having viewed a piece of life.

One might say that Freud was integrating his experiences, developing not a theory but a psychoanalytic view, or point of view, about life and its processes; and this also made him aware of the inadequacy of many of the types of formulations that he had been using. Firstly, I think he was now aware to a great extent that his formulation about dreams was not quite correct: several papers written during the period in which he was treating the Wolf Man add a considerable amount to his recommendations about dream analysis and the clinical use of dreams. Secondly, the theory of narcissism really arose during the course of this man's treatment in the face of the Wolf Man's narcissistic phenomena – particularly his narcissistic identifications with his mother in the menorrhagia and feeling 'I can't go on living like this', and the narcissistic identification with his father mixed up with the old water carrier – his father's heavy breathing. And then there were the perverse tendencies of the little boy: the wish to be beaten and the phantasy of the prince being beaten on the penis, which led on to the paper 'A child is being beaten'. Thirdly, there was the issue of the sexual theories which, when they were based simply on a conception of source, aim and object of instincts, were grossly inadequate. This earlier conception came nowhere near accounting for sexuality in action and people's sexual relationships. It made it sound as if people were simply using one another to masturbate, and did not allow either for any sort of description of the nature of their feelings towards one another or for the problem of jealousy or of masochism which runs so close to the whole question of pleasure and pain.

Now in this area Freud takes a great step forward in describing the primal scene; and he describes it with the intention of viewing it as a great universal organizing phantasy in the sexual development. In a way in this paper there is the preview to the concept of the complete Oedipus complex, as it is later developed in 'The ego and the id' in 1923, and which is the first statement, one might say, of the realities of bisexuality: namely, that there are not just tendencies in the male child that could be equated with passivity, and not just tendencies in the female toward active participation that could be equated with masculinity; rather there really is something very concretely bisexual, male and female: not just active and passive trends but unequivocally male and female, from the very beginning of development, and they both have to find a way of evolving and expressing themselves. The complete Oedipus complex encompasses both the masculine and the feminine Oedipus complex in every individual, boy or girl. Although the truth of this concept was plainly visible to Freud in the Wolf Man, whose femininity is blatant and very strong, one has nevertheless to recognize that Freud does not make the distinction between his femininity and his homosexuality. In consequence, he does not recognize, for example, that the perverse tendencies (such as the desire to be beaten on the penis) and masochistic tendencies are not related to his femininity. He persists in dealing with everything masochistic as if it were passive and thus naturally part of the man's femininity. The patient's identification with his mother and her bleeding was to be equated with wanting to be beaten on the penis.

Nonetheless, a great step forward is clear, for Freud has evolved the foundations of sexual development in concrete and visual form: the basic situation consists of, somewhere, the mother and father having intercourse and, somewhere, the little girl or little boy watching, listening, thinking about it, feeling excited, resentful and whatever else: this is the scene. And it is a great step, for previously, with the talk about impulses, aims and objects, the only approach to emotionality Freud could make was in this rather simple arithmetic: love-turning-into-hate, positive-to-negative, various erotic impulses frustrated and becoming hate impulses, and so on – an approach that barely penetrates the question of affects. But once he has drawn a dramatic scene with dramatis personae in which something is happening in one place, and something else in another place, then the whole thing becomes flooded with feelings and springs to life. He is in a position to examine the emotionality of the situation. The difficulty with the discovery, of course, resides in the indecision as to where the impact comes from, in this equivocation between scene and dream. For Freud comes terribly close in the Wolf Man (much closer than in the Schreber case) to conceptualizing an inner world. If he had just made this step be could have leapt forward the way Melanie Klein's work leapt forward the moment she discovered that children were preoccupied with the inside of their mothers' bodies and the inside of their own bodies and that it was really a place, a world in which life was going on. If Freud could have made that step at this point, there would have been a terrific surge forward that would have led almost immediately to the concept of splitting processes which he could only reach – and even then only very hypothetically – in 1937. But he seems some how unable to come to any such conception at this point; that is, to take the primal scene and find a location for it by placing it inside. And I think the reason was that he just did not have that kind of mind; it took somebody like Mrs Klein, listening to little children talking about the inside of their mother's body with absolute conviction as if it were Budapest or Vienna, as an absolutely geographical place, to realize that there really is an inner world, and that it is not just allegorical or metaphorical, but has a concrete existence – in the life of the mind, not the brain.

The result for Freud is that he is left with this equivocation; in the Schreber case he had equivocated in talking about the world's destruction and could not really come to the conclusion that Schreber smashed the world to pieces because he could not locate this world that had been destroyed. He had to talk about withdrawal of libido and withdrawal of interest instead, and the whole drama is thereby watered down. Now, similarly, in the case of the Wolf Man, it seems to me that because Freud cannot place the primal scene as an internal situation and allow that the impact goes on and on continuously, and because he cannot see the wolf dream (occurring at the age of four) and the other dream (at the age of 23 when he started analysis) as being the same primal scene going on and on inside and still having the same impact on the patient, he therefore cannot

develop a sense of the immediacy of the infantile life. He is left
not only with the equivocation between dream or phantasy and
traumatic factor in the external world, but he is also left with the
necessity of thinking about the analytical work that he is doing
as reconstruction. One has the impression that a large part of
the four years of this patient's analysis was spent analysing this
one dream, although there must have been lots of other dreams
relating to it and throwing light on it, detail after detail. But
because Freud's model was of this reconstructive sort, putting
the jigsaw puzzle together bit by bit and at the end of the paper
talking about the 'solution', his understanding and full use of
the material was handicapped.

I think that the most cogent way of understanding his clinging to the reconstructive nature of the work that he was doing,
is to attribute it to his inability to find a place where it was all
happening in the immediacy of the transference, to see the dream
happening right under his nose. In fact this clinging to the relic
of the archaeological model seems to me to have had the effect
of attenuating the violence and the passion of the transference
situation. And while Freud does speak of the transference as the
past returning and pressing to be put into action, rather than
to be investigated, he does always talk about it as if it were a
relic that returns 'as if' with a lot of feeling. He speaks of the
transference as 'unreal'; and I think one reason for this is that his
attitude towards the countertransference was a very negative one.
He thought of it as an interference with the analyst's work rather
than as a tool: just as when he first recognized the transference he
saw it only as a nuisance. These things are somehow connected
with his reconstructive view, his idea that it was the past returning, and not something present and immediate; because he could
not conceive of a place where it was happening at the moment
and then somehow erupting from that place. For that reason,
the affects connected with it were in a way 'antique' affects: very
precious and very interesting, but not useful in the present, not
alive and vivid at the moment. This of course also affected his
whole view of the nature of the analytic method and its therapeutic effects. As I have said, at first he thought that solving the
riddle, the jigsaw puzzle, and presenting the solution, was the
analyst's work; then in the paper on 'Remembering, repeating

and working through' he states his realization that the analyst's work does not stop there, but also has to help the patient accept the solution and work it through. It is not quite clear what 'working through' means, but at this point – around 1912 – it seems to have some thing of the same significance as his earlier idea that psychopathology was due to experiences or ideas existing in the mind in a sort of foreign-body relationship, unintegrated with other ideas and therefore impossible to be worn away; thus, 'working through' might be otherwise stated as working-away obnoxious ideas and memories.

At this point, the consequence is that the attitude towards the therapy as a method is that it is fairly aggressive towards the patient; and this idea is in keeping with Freud's practice – which might be crudely described as giving the patient the solution and trying to get him to accept it, with the implicit reprimand which he felt toward Irma in the dream of the injection. Callousness of this sort in the attitude to the patient seems to manifest itself toward the Wolf Man in the irrevocable deadline that he gave him, and which probably contributed to his subsequent illness. And this aggressive attitude of 1914 or 1915 turned, by 1936 (when he writes 'Analysis terminable and interminable') into a terribly pessimistic attitude toward the analytic therapy; for here Freud in fact expresses quite a strong feeling of helplessness about the analyst's position: that he really has very little power to influence the patient in any way, but can only offer him the means or tools with which to influence himself. These two attitudes – the aggression and then the pessimism – are more or less opposite sides of the same coin; and they spring, it seems to me, from this relentlessly reconstructive view of the method, in which the analysis is seen to consist of the reconstruction: piecemeal at first, and eventually presented as a whole to the patient; and to find its solution in this. As I have said before, I think Freud was bound to this view because he could not make the step of conceiving of a more immediate and internal situation, of a place inside the mind, in a concrete way; and this was perhaps because he did not have the data for it.

And indeed I think that Freud could not, in any honesty, have made that step, given his material; he could have made it as a feat of imagination, but he was a person who stuck very close to the evidence and he simply did not have any evidence which he could see; and looking back on it, it would have been very difficult to see a concrete inner world. Even Schreber hardly provided it, for his own externalization of psychic reality is so complete that it would have been very hard to put it back into Schreber in one's mind without feeling that you were just imposing your theory and your solution upon him. Little Hans is perhaps a little different: the material about the stork box that he and his sister travelled in, the phantasies of breaking into a place with his father, evidence of claustrophobia and so on, would certainly suggest it. However, it is nothing like the material which Mrs Klein got from two- and three-year-olds when she started working in 1920; they just told her about it. And for some reason – not everybody would have – she took it seriously.

CHAPTER ELEVEN

The child being beaten (the perversions)

T his is the most difficult chapter as far as I am concerned, because it touches on the real watershed period in Freud's work at the end of the First World War, and is followed by the great revolution in his thinking which was to build up during the 1920s and emerge as the Structural Theory. It is the most difficult chapter because it is extremely complicated: the evidence is difficult to comprehend and indeed I do not understand it very well, and so do not expect to be able to clarify it for anyone else. I would begin by emphasizing once more that the approach towards Freud in this book is through his clinical work and his clinical thinking, dealing with his theories – which are expressed as explanatory theories – as having essentially no explanatory power. It seems to me that the approach made to the mind which is based on trying to explain things, is a wrong one, and for this reason I shall take the theories as modes of thought which are intended to be useful in the consulting room and in thinking, writing and talking about one's clinical experience: modes of thought which are intended to gather together, to categorize and to help demonstrate the inter-relationships of the various phenomena that one meets in the consulting room while investigating people's minds. I am going to discuss a watershed period in relation to Freud's modes of thought, and it is very difficult to pick it out in the papers of this time; for we are in effect somewhere between the Wolf Man (whose clinical work was carried out between 1910 and 1914 and written up during the war) and 'Beyond the pleasure principle' of 1920, which contains the seeds of the new Structural Theory. Now while in the development of the concept of the ideal ego into that of the ego-ideal, which I demonstrated in the chapter on *Mourning and Melancholia* and the paper 'On narcissism' , the formation of this Structural Theory was already under way, it was not yet dealt with as such, but rather as an agency in the mind. Freud does not remotely clarify the exact relationship of the structure to the developmental processes, nor easily convey his way of thinking about it. The period was during the war: he was fairly isolated from foreign and German colleagues alike (Ferenczi was in Budapest, Abraham in Berlin) ; the patients he had being few, he was left with a great deal of time for thinking and writing. The result was a group of little but terribly interesting papers; for although he did not write large quantities, what he did set down was absolutely loaded with thought. And it is this evidence of the real struggling that went on at that period that I wish now to try to highlight.

'A child is being beaten' is in my opinion the central paper in this process and will surely form the focal point of this chapter. However, in order to appreciate the full significance of the paper, not just as one on a psychological phenomenon that opened up an entirely new way for the investigation of masochism and therefore of the perversions, but also as embodying Freud's development of new modes of thought, it is necessary to deal with three other papers as well. They are very much more theoretical, and do not make much direct reference to clinical phenomena. In one, which I have already mentioned, on 'Character and anal erotism' (1908), he singles out three character traits – parsimony, stubbornness and orderliness – and for the first time describes the relation between character structure and the development of the libido and fixation of the libido. This was really his first excursion into character. In 1915 there followed 'Instinct and its vicissitudes' (a moralist title), and in 1917, 'Transformations of instincts in relation to anal Erotism'. It seems to me that these two words – 'vicissitudes' and 'transformations' – which I still struggle to understand precisely – are a very important key to the changes in his modes of thinking; and I wish to investigate them a little before going on to 'A child is being beaten'.

Firstly, however, I will recap some of the history up to this point. In the *Studies on Hysteria*, Freud had clearly set about studying simple phenomena (such as amnesia, conversion, anxiety), with the simple theory that they were the result of the repression of certain recollections. This in turn also involved some sort of damming-up of instincts, which were then converted into anxiety; and in turn the anxiety was somehow turned, with the repressed recollections, into symptoms. It was a highly simplistic theory which ran into trouble almost immediately when Freud began extending the field of his study to the obsessional neuroses, for he found that it could not be dealt with purely on the basis of recollections. Somehow the affects became detached from these, with the result that the recollections were not repressed but the affects were: the recollections were available for memory but the affects had disappeared; he found that indeed it was pretty mysterious. He was quite convinced that it had something to do with sexuality and, discovering a great deal of confirmation for infantile sexuality in the course of his clinical work, that the Oedipus Complex as the central conflict situation in development was ubiquitous. Moreover, he was convinced that the whole thing was developmental, originating not in later life, but in infancy. Then came the case of Little Hans, which provided such lovely confirmation of the actual existence of the Oedipus Complex and of the infantile neurosis in children. The Rat Man case helped him to understand that there was conflict involved, and that it was conflict between love and hate in some way in the obsessional neurosis, not just conflict between ideas and desires that were unacceptable to the outside world and social standards. Then, as I said in connection with the Leonardo case, one can see that his ideas about psychoanalysis were expanding to try to accommodate the conception of a person's life as a unified thing which could be studied in a linear way from its beginning to its end, a continuous development in which progress and regression and other processes all had their place and were linked together in an integrated history. In the Schreber case, Freud seemed to discover that not only was there such a thing as a life, but there was such a thing as a world; and that everybody lived his life in his world, and that his world was in some way partly his own conception and in some way the world of his own particular mind, able to fall to pieces or to be torn or battered to pieces; he also seemed to discover that terrible things happen to a person when he has allowed his world to thus disintegrate.

So gradually the whole concern became something which could reasonably be thought of as a unified field of psychology, related to personality and personality development. At the same time in history, of course, other schools of psychology were growing up that were studying the same or different phenomena. The Gestalt school was studying psychology from an entirely different point of view, very phenomenological but having nothing to do with development and fundamentally nothing to do with personality. Other schools were much more sociological or anthropological in their orientation. But Freud pulled his own work together under the firm net of psychology with these four different categories: studying the developmental process and its genetics; studying its topography (that is, levels of consciousness and problems related to this: as he thought then, the crucial question related to psychopathology) ; the question of dynamics (that is, mechanisms of the mind by which the psychic energies were manipulated) ; and the economic aspect (that is, the attempt to define its quantitative aspects). At that time, by 'quantitative', Freud was meaning 'psychic energy', which he was then thinking of as a very concrete concern as if it were electricity or hydrostatic energy or heat. Therefore, the nature of Freud's modes of thought stemmed from this essentially hydrostatic energetics model; and his concepts related to affects were also almost purely quantitative, conceived of in terms of quantities of excitation in the mind. As the phenomenology that he and other people began to study extended beyond obsessional neurosis and the whole realm of narcissistic phenomena came into play in its relation to more serious illnesses such as manic-depressive states or schizophrenia, or hypochondria, it became increasingly clear that his modes of thought were just not tying the ends together and were not providing useful tools for comprehending the clinical phenomena. By this time the transference in the consulting room was no longer being dealt with merely as a resistance, but considered as something in its own right. This is evident to a certain extent in the Rat Man case, but still more clearly so in the Wolf Man, where the transference was seen as a communication with its own particular level of validity. And although it was still being used mainly for the purpose of reconstruction, this latter was no longer the simple serial delineation of a chain of mental events running back to a traumatic experience or a repressed incident that it had been in the early days, but had become (as seen in Leonardo and the Wolf Man case) an attempt to reconstruct a life and the entire development of a person: his personality, his interests, his relationships.

Now by 1915, Freud had finished with the Wolf Man case, but I think that nevertheless it remained the crucial case in his subsequent development; he was busy writing it up and thinking about it, and at this time he was still very bound up with the Libido Theory. This is expressed very clearly in the paper 'Instincts and their vicissitudes' (1915). What Freud means by the term 'vicissitudes' at this point, seems to be somehow connected with the context of a person's whole development: his character, his symptoms, what is healthy as well as what is ill about him. The 'vicissitudes of instinct' seem to mean something standing in specific relation to phases of development. Along with Abraham, he was thinking of personality development in terms of a series of organizations: and these organizations were at this point thought of as pregenital and genital. The pregenital organization was already considered to have different phases: oral- and (as Abraham was already thinking) anal-sadistic, as well as oral- and anal-erotic; but the main division was between pregenital and genital. Pregenital was also thought of as being the realm *par excellence* of narcissism – this latter currently being considered by and large in these libido terms: that is, narcissism as a stage in the development of the deployment of the libido from auto-erotism to object relations in which the body of the person was taken as the object of the libidinal impulses, and then going on to object relations in which the bodies of other people are chosen as the object of the libidinal (i.e. primarily the sexual) impulses. Now the term 'vicissitudes' seems to have its roots of meaning in such a question as, 'What happens to the pregenital organization when development proceeds to the genital organization?' Where does it go? Obviously the erogenous zones are still there, the stimulation is still there, the phantasies and desires connected with it must be still somewhere in the mind: what happens to it? The answers to this seem to be given in terms of the ways in which the libido can be manipulated. And Freud thought of these manipulations at that point in a way that is fairly identical with 'defence mechanisms' as it has come to be used later in psychoanalytic history. He names these four in the paper: turning into its opposite, turning against the self, repression and sublimation; discussing not the last two since he has talked about them a lot before, but mainly the first two. And he does not use 'self' here as a technical term as we use it today (meaning a portion of the personality that has the meaning of 'self ' and which contains both ego and id components integrated in some functional way); he is using the term in a purely descriptive way.

In order to understand the idea of an instinct having vicissitudes of these four sorts, one has to understand that Freud was thinking of instincts as having qualities that tend to come in pairs; and the major pairs were the instincts relating to love and hate (that is, having the affects of love and hate connected with them): that of sadism and masochism, and that of activity and passivity. There is also the pair of masculine and feminine, but this he still reserves for the genital organization, not thinking of pregenital masculinity or pregenital femininity, but only of active and passive. Therefore, by the term 'inverting' an instinct into its opposite, Freud meant, for instance, that the instinct containing the affect of love can be converted into the instinct containing the affect of hate; similarly a sadistic impulse or instinct can be inverted into a masochistic one. He did not explain how it comes about, but simply said that this is something which can happen. Therefore, the turning-against-the-self is the equivalent of a return to narcissism: that is, the diversion of libido back into the self and making it into narcissistic libido. This is what Freud means by 'vicissitudes of instinct' at this point. He is still bound by the Libido Theory and to the idea that the explanation of human behaviour (for he is still trying to explain things) and of human feelings is to be found in the deployment of instinct; and the deployment of instinct is governed by these mechanisms or vicissitudes.

Two years later he was to write a paper called 'On transformations of instincts'; and I do not think that from these titles alone, one could tell why 'vicissitudes' and 'transformations' may not be interchangeable as descriptive terms. The fact is that in a very subtle way an entirely different mode of thought has come to be operative in his mind: and what he describes mainly in this paper concerns the anal instincts: the instincts connected with the anal erogenous zone and therefore essentially connected with the relationship of the anus and rectum to the faecal mass, and its meaning, significance and phantasy implications. It concerns the variety of ways in which this anal impulse relates itself to the faecal mass, of ways that have different meanings not clearly distinguished or differentiated from one another; and these meanings are, in essence, enumerated as follows (in what might now be called a 'confusional series'): faeces–penis–baby–money or gift. Now it is not at all clear why this is being called a transformation of instinct; for it does not seem to do anything to the instinct at all; it seems to do something to the way in which the instinct is conceived, and the meaning which is attributed to the action of the instinct: that is, whether the anal impulses and the anal excitements and phantasies are experienced as related to a faecal mass that has the meaning of penis or baby or faeces.

This, to my mind, is the beginning of ego psychology and tolls the death of the Libido Theory. I am sure many people would not agree with me, but I think that it dies at about this time, being replaced by ego psychology and object relations psychology – which are really the same thing, although they are talked about as if they were deadly enemies. Thus in moving away (quite decisively in this instance) from one mode of thought, Freud has moved towards another that is going to have a much greater organizing power in linking together phenomena, bringing them into understandable – as opposed to explicable – relation to one another. He has moved from thinking of instincts as simply body tensions requiring satisfaction (with the implication that happiness is something equivalent to a pleasant comatose state, so becoming known as the Nirvana Principle), to considering the mind as functioning primarily in relation to the manipulation of meaning. This movement away from an energetics principle, on to the study of the mind as an instrument for the manipulation of meaning, seems to me – as I said before – the beginning of ego and object relations psychology. And this is what we practise today.

It is interesting with reference to this that the only place (to my belief) in which the word 'energy', taken from the First Law of Thermodynamics, is replaced by the word 'entropy' taken from the Second Law of Thermodynamics, comes toward the end of the Wolf Man case. At this point Freud is using it in application to what might be called the stickiness of the libido: that is, the difficulty that people have in shifting their cathexes, their attachments, their interests, altering the balance of what is valuable and important in their lives. He is therefore talking about entropy as something essentially equivalent to inertia. But I think that it is a very important step in his thinking; for, with the help of information theory and linguistic philosophy, it has led to the development of our use of the idea of entropy. It is no longer peculiar to physics, describing energy running down or becoming unavailable as stated in the Second Law of Thermodynamics, but has been extended to include organization in general, and the progress from chaos to order. Now it seems to me that this is something that permeates and quite alters Freud's thinking from this point onwards. Although the trappings of the Libido Theory remain, and the language of cathexis, transformations of energies, hypercathexis and so on, still continues, yet the underlying mode of thought seems to me to have made a dramatic shift. The terms are no longer energy and its deployment, but meaning and the organization of meaning from chaotic modes of thought to organized and harmonious modes of thought. It is towards this that psychoanalysis has been directing its attention and development ever since.

While the little paper 'On transformations of instincts' (1917), mentioned above, is based on these astute clinical observations about the lack of differentiation in the deployment or organization of the pregenital and, particularly, the anal organization of the meaning and significance of the faeces (as penis, babies), it is primarily a theoretical paper. Our first glimpse of this new mode of thought actually being employed clinically is in the marvellous little paper entitled 'A child is being beaten'. I feel I should preface my discussion of it by saying that no patient has ever said to me 'a child is being beaten', nor do I know of anyone else whose patient has said this: yet many of Freud's patients seem to have told him that they had this phantasy. It must have been a 19th-century phenomenon. Freud himself very interestingly points out that it does not in fact seem to be a phenomenon that can be traced back to a specific factor of children being beaten more in those days, or beaten more in Germany, or in Vienna, amongst the middle class, or amongst Jewish people; indeed the people who had this phantasy were generally middle-class people who had not been beaten and whose upbringing had been gentle.

But although we do not often meet with the phenomenon as such in practice these days, we do of course meet with plenty of beating phantasies, beating perversions and flagellist fetishism. I would think the evidence is fairly convincing that the phantasy that 'a child is being beaten' – meaning, fundamentally, beaten to death – lies somewhere at the root of sexual perversions. Freud himself also comes to this conclusion: that is, that where you meet masochism you will somewhere find the phantasy that 'a child is being beaten'. Now this approach to masochism is entirely different from the one which had formerly been expressed in the 1915 paper on the 'Vicissitudes of instinct'. At that point he was talking about masochism as the turning-against-the-self of a sadistic impulse.

But at this point he is investigating the transformations of a phantasy that 'a child is being beaten': whether the 'child being beaten' is the subject himself, or some other child; whether it is a male or a female child; whether it is being beaten by the father or the mother; whether it is a loved or a hated child? In short, what is the significance of the phantasy? He compares the experience he has had with male patients who have had this phantasy to that with female patients, tracing it to three different stages. In a way he does tie himself up in terrific knots about it; it is extremely interesting and very confusing. However, what eventually emerges – and this Freud pinpoints very clearly – is that the most important thing is the relationship of the phantasy to masochism: namely, that 'the child being beaten' is, at a certain stage in the transformation of this phantasy, the patient himself or herself. He then relates it back to the phantasy in the Wolf Man where the prince was beaten on the penis, and also to the man's masochistic anal tendencies as expressed in his need for colonic irrigations and so on. He relates it to a certain extent to his phobia of the wolf, tracing it – as he had previously done – to the fact that his fear of the wolf was related to his desire to be copulated with by his father and to his desire to be castrated and made into a female.

When one returns to that paper in the light of 'A child is being beaten' and in the light of this shift from 'vicissitudes' to 'transformations' of instincts, you discover that there are two highly significant statements in it, which, to my mind, foreshadow the whole development of Freud's re-thinking about sexuality and sexual perversions: this great shift from energetics and distribution of the libido, to ego functions and thinking and dreaming. The two statements which are in a sense absolutely modern are: firstly, the defining of the phantasy, in relation to the Wolf Man's sexual peculiarities, to the effect that, in copulation, a person may be identified with a person inside the mother being copulated with by the father; the intercourse may have the meaning for him that he is really the baby inside being copulated with; and secondly, that a man may be identified with his own penis as a baby that is getting inside the mother. Of course, we are still today and have been for the last twenty years, studying precisely this kind of thing: namely, the way in which infantile phantasies are related to the inside of the mother's body. As I said, these two statements are highly significant in that they are, to my mind, the precursors of a mighty leap in the dark by Freud: to deal with the perversions as very complicated structures; to deal with the sexual life as filled with meaning rather than simply devoted to the mechanics of gaining satisfaction for instinctual tensions; to conceive the complexity of the phantasies that may underlie what descriptively may be called an ordinary act of sexual intercourse. Furthermore, one might put these two statements together: that of the person being identified with the baby inside the woman being copulated with by its father, and the person being identified with his own penis as the baby getting back into the mother's body or back into the womb; and one might see these in conjunction as a phantasy by which Freud has conceived of a sexual act, in which the entrance of the penis into the vagina is the child getting into the mother, and subsequently being copulated with there by the father's penis.

Now Freud does not make any specific reference to this in the paper 'A child is being beaten', and we have to wait for a few years until he returns to the problem of masochism in 1924 with 'The economic problem of masochism'. But we should keep in mind that he has already described these phantasies here in the Wolf Man; that he has already made this shift from talking about vicissitudes of instinct and the energetics of their deployment, to transformations of instinct and transformations of the meaning of the act or behaviour or relationship. One can see that he has made a very great step forward in his approach to sexuality. Formerly (as I have said) one would always have had to complain that his description of sexuality considered it as in essence a meaningless act, in no way differentiated from any other act for gratifying the body – scratching it, eating a plum or whatever – other than that it was the most convenient way, much better than masturbating. In other words, there had been nothing in his theory about sexuality to bring meaning into the relationship of the two people who were engaged in it. Now he has introduced into the whole field of sexuality rich possibilities for investigating the meaning.

Now of course one can object that this is what he has been doing all along; and indeed it is what he has been doing all along. If one goes back to the Dora case, or to the *Studies on Hysteria*, one will see that, as Freud says, they do indeed sound like short stories; he has been investigating the meaning all along. But to be investigating something and describing its phenomenology is a very different thing from having the conceptual tools with which to organize these phenomena so that they take on the significance of a body of knowledge which can then be passed on to somebody else for use in his consulting room. What an exciting and important period this is! It was made possible by his having a lot of time on his hands to think about the problems that were troubling him. And the problem which troubled him most at this time seems to have been the paradoxical one of masochism. It was paradoxical to Freud because it did not conform in any way to his central economic concept about pain; for the whole Libido Theory really rested on the concept that excessive stimulation, internal or external, was experienced as unpleasure or pain, and that relief of tension was experienced as pleasure or less unpleasure. Within the confines of that formulation, there was no way at all of accounting for masochism; that is, for the pleasure in being the object of the sadistic, pain-provoking behaviour of other people. Now even in 'A child is being beaten', Freud does not make much progress with the problem of masochism itself. True, he pinpoints it in the series of transformations of the phantasy from 'a child is being beaten' to 'a child that I hate is being beaten', to 'I am being beaten by my father'; and somewhere in this transformation, the phantasy that 'I am loved by my father because he is beating that other child' somehow turns into 'I am loved by my father because he is beating me'. But there Freud is still just on the verge of recognizing something that has to do with identification processes.

And indeed he has constantly been on the verge of this ever since he began talking about Leonardo's homosexuality based on his identification with his mother and loving a young boy the way his mother loved him; since he began talking about Schreber's identification with his wife and how lovely it must be to be a woman being copulated with, and his relation to God as a woman; he has been on the verge of it all through the Wolf Man, in talking about the Wolf Man's identification with his mother's menorrhagia, and his identification with his sister with regard to the incident of his weeping at Pushkin's grave. In *Mourning and Melancholia* of course, he is constantly on the verge of it, in raising the question of who is really in pain: is it the ego berating the ego-ideal or is it the ego ideal berating the ego? And he almost brings it all together in this paper, in trying to investigate this paradox about mental pain. This seems to me to be one of the main obstacles preventing him from being quite satisfied with the Libido Theory as an explanatory one: for quite evidently masochism could not be explained in accordance with it.

The previous formulation of instinct-turning-against-the-self used in the paper on the 'Vicissitudes of instinct' is simply a sleight of hand, and does not satisfy any requirements since it does not describe the process in any way, but merely puts the words to it. To define masochism as 'sadism turning against the self ' is easy enough, but it does not actually say anything about it. In 'A child is being beaten', Freud comes close to recognizing the central masochistic phantasy that 'I am identified with a child who is being beaten by my father because he loves me and hates that other child.' The identification is implicit. And when one couples that with those two statements from the Wolf Man about the copulation with a child inside the mother's body, you catch a glimpse of a process that Freud has almost grasped: so that instead of 'My father copulating with that child', 'My father beating that child', one should understand 'I am that child and I am being copulated with by my father in that painful beating way because he loves me.' There is masochism.

CHAPTER TWELVE

Beyond the pleasure principle and group psychology (the ego-ideal)

This chapter brings us to the very verge of 'The ego and the id' and the Structural Theory, which represents such an immense change in the conceptual tools with which psychoanalysts can try to understand and organize the clinical phenomena. In order to understand the importance of this change it is essential to see in what way Freud was in difficulty, both clinically and conceptually, and how he was struggling to find a way out of it. 'Beyond the pleasure principle' and 'Group psychology' each in their own way attempt to solve the problem. Freud always, as he himself says, attempts to take the citadel by storm; and each of these papers endeavours to do everything at once. The first attempts to solve the problem by taking the Libido Theory and, as it were, standing it up on its ear: as if a change simply in the nature of the duality of instincts (giving them different names and a different type of significance) would solve everything. The second attempts the solution by establishing a concept of the ego ideal, which later of course in 'The ego and the id' turns into that of the super-ego. And both go some distance to enrich the conceptual tools with which he worked, as I now hope to explain.

In order to do this one has first to realize the nature of his trouble, and the kind of clinical phenomena for which his theoretical tools provided no help in comprehending or organizing. The main problem is that of mental pain, with which he had never had a satisfactory way of dealing conceptually, primarily because he was anchored to the neurophysiological conception of mental pain as a quantitative rather than a qualitative matter, as something having a quasi-physical significance, but no meaning. From the *Project* onward, he has always thought of mental pain as unpleasure, and anchored it to such conceptions as Fechner's 'constancy principle' (later called the Nirvana principle), and other quasi-neurophysiological conceptions, which reduced the aim of mental life to something equivalent to semi-coma: directed towards the reduction of mental tensions to a minimum, in a kind of stuporous comfort. Of course Freud knew this was wrong, but he could not find any way around it without jettisoning the whole conception that had been the inspiration of his younger days, in establishing a scientific psychology; and 'scientific' in the Germanic framework meant explaining things; and explaining things meant demonstrating causal relationships; and this in turn required quantitative statements. All statements other than quantitative (poetic, artistic) were fanciful, and therefore not scientific. A work like 'Beyond the pleasure principle' is a rather beautiful example of this split in Freud between the clinician struggling with the phenomena of the mind and their meaning, and the scientific theorizer trying to present a scientific theory which explains everything.

This then is the first of his difficulties: concerning the problem of mental pain and the question of affects and feelings, emotions, which had no place in his theory because they were dealt with as essentially meaningless, as by-products or the efflorescences of mental processes. Associated with this, he was in difficulty because his great economic principle was the pleasure principle, which more or less stated that pleasure consisted of the reduction of tensions, and unpleasure consisted of the increase or perhaps (he sometimes thought) their rate or acceleration of increase. But many phenomena made it quite clear to him that the attainment of pleasure and the avoidance of pain was not a satisfactory economic principle, in that it only covered a range of phenomena which could be subsumed under the category of wish-fulfilment (as in the dream theory). And many things going on in the mind simply could not be subsumed in that way. In 'Beyond the pleasure principle' he tries to bring together these puzzling phenomena.

We have already heard about masochism; and Freud has already gone some distance toward coming to grips with it, through the recognition that the puzzle of masochism (like the puzzle of melancholia) involved a question such as 'Whose pain is it?', and that identification processes were involved in some way. But raising that question did not go any distance towards coping with certain other phenomena; and the one which came to the forefront at this time during the war, when there were so many cases of 'shell-shock', traumatic neuroses and so on, was the phenomenon of the traumatic dream. This seemed the ultimate example to absolutely flaunt the pleasure principle, even when modified by the so-called reality principle.

The traumatic neuroses exhibited the following phenomenon: that the person dreamed over and over again of the situation of terror that had precipitated his breakdown: in battle or expectation of battle; as a result of explosions near them or without any explosion near them. The apparently ceaseless repetition of these dreams and the patient's waking in terror simply could not be subsumed under the dream theory about wish fulfilment, nor under the anxiety dream theory, in which the mechanisms for creating hallucinatory wish fulfilment were inadequate and the anxiety broke through. These dreams could not fall under that category, because they seemed to have no resemblance at all to dream structure: they seemed in their content to be simple factual repetitions of the experience or the expected experience that precipitated the breakdown. So they appeared to represent a phenomenon entirely different from any with which his dream theory had attempted to cope.

Freud had also noticed by this time that along with the repetitiveness of these particular dreams, went another phenomenon: namely the repetitiveness in children's play, and their endless desire for the repetition of the same story, the same game, the same experience in the minutest detail without modification. He suggested in this paper that there might be a more primitive economic principle (which is what he means by 'beyond' the pleasure principle: going back to the primitive mental processes beyond the establishment of that principle): a principle beyond this, which he called the repetition compulsion. This compulsion to repeat became linked with that other phenomenon which he had already called the 'compulsion to repeat' in relation to the transference: in which the transference as a phenomenon in the analytic setting seemed to manifest an inherent compulsion to repeat the events of childhood, in particular those events to which fixation had occurred, or which were traumatic experiences. From 'compulsion to repeat' to 'repetition compulsion' required only an inversion of language. And at the beginning of this paper it was these three phenomena which he brought together in order to formulate the idea that, at the most primitive levels of instinct, the instincts manifest an economic principle which is in essence a mindless compulsion to repeat: to repeat in a sense that is 'beyond' the pleasure principle, that is, having nothing to do with questions of pleasure or pain, but being simply the tendency to repeat endlessly the experience by which an instinct has manifested itself in the primitive organization of the child's mind and relationships.

Up to this point, 'Beyond the pleasure principle' is a very clinical paper in which Freud has been trying to make these three clinical phenomena coalesce: the transference, the dreams of traumatic neurosis, and the play of children; and in this part of the paper occurs the famous passage about the child playing with the cotton-reel. It has been up to now a paper dealing with clinical phenomena and enunciating an economic principle which may possibly be of use in trying to understand certain phenomena of the mind not approachable by means of the other economic principles – the pleasure principle and its modification in respect of external reality, the reality principle. One might say that here, the psychoanalytic part of the paper ends: and it swings back to the *Project* of 1897. The rest of it is an extremely elaborate speculation (Freud admits that it is highly speculative and even seems embarrassed about it) about the origins of life and the origins of sexuality and the way in which this compulsion to repeat is really the compulsion to repeat an inorganic state, and is therefore a death instinct. In other words, the instinct which he had previously been calling a life-preservative one is really (by a most tortuous tautological argument) the instinct to find one's own way to death, rather than being interfered with by others by being murdered on the way. And in effect the argument amounts to this: that a so called life-preservative instinct (with its element of conservation) is now to be called a 'death instinct'. In a sense its significance does not change, except that it is now being seen as a primary destructive impulse in which the aim is to destroy all the bonds linking together the cellular elements of the organism, and reduce them to an inorganic state – a sort of definition of death. In opposition to this, the sexual instincts are now to be called Eros or the 'life instinct', and to be seen as a constructive factor bringing together living units and making them into ever greater and more complicated structures, able to take on more complex functions. In none of this are the emotions of love and hate mentioned, the emotions accompanying Eros and Thanatos (as it is called by Freud later on); again emotions are left out of the theory and therefore, given that there is a difference between meaning and significance, the meaning is also excluded. Freud enunciates the significance of a life instinct which is constructive, building greater units; and a death instinct which destructively tears them down, reducing life to an inorganic state; but of course this says nothing about the meaning which these processes have as they manifest themselves in mental life. Therefore it can be (and is) linked with biology and the behaviour of the protozoa; with the *Project*'s scheme for the distribution of excitations and the reduction of tensions to a minimum; with the constancy principle and the Nirvana principle. The paper ends up with a theory implicitly linking itself to all these. And at the end of 'Beyond the pleasure principle', one is left in the dark as to how to make use of this formulation – of either the compulsion to repeat, or the life and death instinct, which is not supposed to mean anything very different from the life-preservative and sexual instincts, except in so far as it gives them a more biological foundation.

In one sense, however, 'Beyond the pleasure principle' is a great triumph, in that Freud has moved in the direction of rescuing violence, destructiveness and cruelty from a position of being tucked away in sexuality as a component instinct called sadism – having no necessary part in human life except in response to frustration, deprivation, or seduction. It is a great move forward, incorporating a conceptual vessel in which the meaning of primary destructiveness as an instinctual force is given a place, with the possibility of subsuming cruelty, violence, sado-masochism and perversity under the instinctual category; giving it a status in which (like the House of Lords) it has some say in the matter though not in the running of the country. Then the sexual instinct Eros is placed in opposition to it with the implication that it is going to win the day until senility sets in. This is more or less the picture one receives from Freud's attitude towards these two instincts: the death instinct exists, and its aim is to lead the organism through its life history to its natural death. But in this paper there is no picture of a continual conflict between life and death or love and hate, creativeness and destructiveness; because the whole concern is placed in the context of bound cathexes and floating cathexes, and the way in which the destructive instinct is turned outward and away from its primary masochism, primary self-destructiveness; and projected. It therefore evaporates, and nothing much is changed by this paper except for the creation of a conceptual framework which Freud will begin to use functionally in later papers. In a way, however, he never made much of it; and I think never took it very seriously as a major modification of his viewpoint about mental functioning. It seems to me that Freud's view about life and death instincts was that they provided a neater and more inclusive way of talking about sexual and life preservative instincts, owing to the wider coverage provided. Thus this new economic principle of the repetition phenomenon, provided a canopy under which the phenomena of masochism, the transference, and traumatic neuroses could all be gathered. Imagining oneself as an analyst in 1920, however, one would not have known what to do with this principle, apart from having this slightly neater framework for discussion. And indeed everyone was terribly confused about life-preservative and sexual instincts: about how the life-preservative instinct could also be narcissistic and the sexual instinct could turn back on to the self as narcissism, and the two then seem to flow together; no-one could really tell where the other phenomena of violence, ambivalence and destructiveness, fitted in. But it is a fascinating exposition of this split with which I have been concerned; although I think that it is by this stage very much diminished;

and although his enthusiasm is reminiscent of the boyish enthusiasm of the Fliess letters, he is also embarrassed and troubled
about it, saying, in effect, 'now this is speculation ... maybe next
week some biologist will come up with something making it all
sound like nonsense', but that 'anyway we must speculate, and
not be bound ...'. It is in this way very different from the *Project*,
making very nice and interesting reading; it does not seem to
have done any harm to psychoanalysis – except that a great deal
of Lilliputian debate has raged over the question of the life and
death instincts; much psychoanalytic politics has been staged in
this tiny bit of territory.

The next paper, 'Group psychology', is a different matter;
because it is the first paper in which Freud really tried to come to
grips with the problem of identification. As I have said, this has
been touched on time and again throughout his writings; yet it
is virtually never mentioned in the index though you may look
through volume after volume, except in relation to *Mourning and
Melancholia*; even in the Leonardo paper where the identification with his mother is absolutely essential, it is not in the index;
nor in the 'Wolf Man'. The omission is quite correct, for he was
using the term descriptively, and not conceptually as yet. Up to
this point identification has not really been a concept: not until
this paper, when it is given some space and described at some
length. In this very interesting paper Freud goes to work on all
sorts of things, from the Church to the Army to falling in love
to hypnosis to entropy to the problem of group formation and
leadership and identification processes. What he is really working toward is trying to give some shape to the concept of the
ego ideal, which he began to formulate back in the paper 'On
narcissism', and then in *Mourning and Melancholia*. He realized
that he had no definitive way of formulating it because he could
not quite tell what it was that brought it about. Already he was
talking about the ego and the separating-off of a part of the ego as
a result of the process of introjection. This resulted in identification by a process analogous to eating one's father (i.e. cannibalis-
tic) – although it was unclear whether he was eaten before or after
he died. Freud could not quite achieve a formulation of what
happened. A figure was seen as introjected into the ego, and then
somehow this part of the ego was separated off to function as an

ideal or love object for the rest of the ego. Some sort of spatial concept lay behind it. In this paper on group psychology he comes as close as he ever does in any of his writings to describing an inner world. For relating this introjection of an object into the ego, he connects it with the relinquishment of the relationship with the object in the outside world, until the whole operation of the object relationship is transferred to this new stage, on which the whole drama is re-enacted: the ego presenting itself as a love-object to the ego-ideal, aspiring to become like it. In the background is always the lesson of *Melancholia*: that the whole process may turn sour and the participants start scolding and hating one another; or the ego may rebel against being scolded and expel the ego ideal, triumphing over it in its new freedom and becoming very manic. By this time Abraham had already begun to think that mania was connected with some sort of anal expulsion: getting rid of this introjected object or ego-ideal and triumphing over it, treating it like faeces; Freud was very fascinated by this idea, and began to realize it as something very active going on in some place: yet he could never quite formulate that it really was a 'place'; instead he speaks about 'imago', which seems to mean something equivalent to 'prototype', and again hedges the question of concreteness. This is, however, where he comes most close to describing what would later be called an 'inner world' in a concrete sense, in which internal objects and introjected objects have a life that stands in relation to the ego as external objects stand in relation to the personality or self.

The content of this paper concerns the understanding of group psychology; this is where Freud talks about the primal horde and the murder and eating of the father, and the competition between males for the sexual possession of the women; and where he places his theory about the origins of religion as an addendum to *Totem and Taboo*. This is the main purpose of the paper, yet what is of greatest interest to psychoanalytic history, is this first organized description of the ego ideal and discussion about identifications. Now with identifications he does not seem to make much headway. He had already spoken of narcissistic identifications and of identification by introjection; and that distinction between regressive identifications (as he also calls them) and progressive ones is somehow lost here in favour of 'primitive' or 'primary' identifications, in which identification is seen as a very primitive process occurring naturally at the very beginnings of life, when identification and object relationship are indistinguishable from one another. He makes no attempt to explain how that comes about; again he implies (I suppose) that it is an inherent capacity, as it were 'beyond narcissism', earlier than narcissism, in which objects are identified with, or not distinguished from, the self. This may be what he means by 'primary narcissism', but it is never very clear.

Then there is a later form of identification which is specifically related to the relinquishment of an object in the outside world, and the introjection of this object into the ego, and the separating-off of the part of the ego which contains this object; which separated-off portion assumes ego ideal function, or becomes the ego ideal. Freud is at this point talking almost exclusively about the father, and really only about the boy's relationship to the father and his introjection and identification. He states very clearly that this identification by introjection to form the separated-off portion of the ego called the ego ideal, is an identification very different in quality from the primitive form of identification in which the object is simply not recognized as separate, and the identification with it and experience of some identity with it is an immediate experience. He makes it quite clear that introjective identification, on the other hand, is an experience of confrontation with an admired object, which arouses aspirations and desires for emulation and development. This is very important; and although in this paper Freud does not penetrate very far into the nature of these types of identification (he is not really greatly interested in primary identification), yet he does distinguish between them.

Certain other aspects of this paper are worth noticing. He talks about hypnosis and more clearly than at any time since the *Three Essays*, about falling in love. It is important that his conception of sexual gratification is that it loosens object relationships; and the relinquishment of sexual aims or inhibited sexuality makes for durable and rich relationships. This has a rather cynical ring, but I think that Freud does not mean it to be cynical. He was thinking of sexuality in these energic terms; and since he was still bound to the energy theory at this time, it 'followed' (not as a matter of observation, but as a logical continuation of the implications of the Libido Theory) that once your libido has been discharged you feel fine and have no need of any further relationship with anyone until the tensions build up again. Just as sexual gratification is seen to deplete the ego of its vitality or tension, thereby releasing its tension and diminishing its need for an object, so is falling in love described as something which depletes the ego of narcissistic cathexis, and all the capacity for cathexis (that is, for relatedness and interest – for it is often defined as interest) is turned outward. Freud asserts that it does absolutely necessitate overestimation and idealization of the love object, and that it is equivalent to a state of enthralment or some very pathological state of mind, which he then equates with hypnosis and the relationship of the members of a group to its leader. And though this sounds cynical and repulsive, yet one has to remember that in this theoretical context Freud is not talking about life, but rather about cathexes and libido – a different matter altogether. This then was the position in 1920 or 1921. To this point the change in the instinct theory does not effectively give new meaning to anything; it simply provides new vessels for containing the concept of instinct, without adding much to their clinical usefulness. Freud has clarified to some extent the concept of identification and the ego-ideal, in the paper on 'Group psychology', with the separating-off from the ego of a special component; but he has not given the definition any sharpness because he is fundamentally uncertain about the central problem of the assimilation of an object into the ego, which seems to miscarry in some way. He cannot locate it exactly; he may refer to a 'stage', but cannot wholeheartedly accept it as a real stage with real actors upon it, and is therefore still in difficulty about giving it the concreteness which would truly set the inner world apart as independent from (though analogous to) relationships to objects in the outside world.

CHAPTER THIRTEEN

The ego and the id (the advent of the structural theory)

hen one attempts to take stock of the position of
Freud's thought at this time, and to juxtapose it
to the clinical data with which he was struggling,
two basic factors present the selves. One is the residue of the
Project, demanding restatement in terms of the new clinical
phenomena; and at the other extreme there is evidence of the
operation on his thought of the two masses of clinical data in
his experience comprised in the Wolf Man and in Schreber's
extraordinary diary. One sees on the one hand his tendency
to 'take the citadel by storm' and this by means to reduce
the mysteries of nature to academic order and obedience;
and on the other, his respect for an apparent galaxy of clinical phenomena thrown up by the psychoanalytical method,
which defied such tyranny.

What were these phenomena? Schreber's hypochondria and
persecutory delusions had revealed the world of narcissism,
which Freud was seeing primarily in terms of the ego taking its
own body as sexual object. By withdrawing cathexis from external objects on to the ego, early types of identification processes
were invoked which antedated object relations. These could

later be regressed to as fixation points (the stage of narcissism which followed auto-erotism in the baby's development). Then Schreber's 'world destruction' phantasy revealed the fact that in the mind a 'subjective world' is built up during development, from the 'sublimations and identifications' of the ego. The crumbling of this world was viewed by Freud as a relatively slow, non-violent process, resulting from the withdrawal of the libido from objects in the outside world. Just why this should produce a catastrophe in dementia or schizophrenia and not in melancholia he could not say, for he viewed the withdrawal of libido to be the primary operation in both situations. In any case, Freud saw this crumbling of the world of the mind as the event underlying the chaotic confusion of the dementia, from which a type of recovery was effected by building a delusional world from the fragments, 'not more splendid but at least one he could live in'.

This uncertainty, this hovering between 'sublimations' and 'identifications' as the foundation of character, is further illustrated in Freud's handling of the data of the Wolf Man, and appears to embody his uncertainty in abandoning the Libido Theory in favour of a more structural conception of the mind and mental events. The emergence in his thought of a 'special gradient in the Ego', a specialized part of the mind, at first called an 'ideal ego' and later on 'ego ideal', leaned towards a structuralization of ego-functions. He at first attributed such varied functions as censorship, the setting of aspirations, reality testing and self-observation to this part of the mind, and saw it as being in some way linked to identification processes in melancholia. But he was undecided as to whether the alteration was in the ego itself: to which the abandoned object cathexis fell as an introjection – the 'shadow of the object' in melancholia and the 'radiance of the object' in mania; or whether it formed something quite separate from the ego. Did the ego-ideal rant against the ego identified with the ambivalently held object, or did the ego rail against the object which it had abandoned externally by setting it up in the inside of the mind?

Since Freud's new theory of life- and death-instincts moved him toward perceiving conflicts of a new order, between the two classes of instincts and their derivatives rather than between adherence to the pleasure principle and the demands of reality, he realized that his central preoccupation with levels of consciousness was no longer either so mysterious or so crucial. Furthermore this topographic theory had run into great difficulties of a semantic nature, which Freud was at some trouble to sort out in 'The ego and the id'. At least three different uses of the term 'unconscious' could be recognized: a purely descriptive one – related to mental phenomenology; a dynamic one connected with the theory of repression (which was already being broadened into the theory of the mechanisms of defence of which repression was perhaps of less importance than originally thought); and thirdly, a systematic usage. This last had been a move in the direction of structuralizing the model of the mind; as had, along with it, the conceptions of the stages of organization of the libido, which Freud and Abraham had been working out. But the mixture of topographic systems and developmental organizations did not coalesce into a unified theory; especially as Freud was now keenly aware that the 'unconscious' and the 'repressed' could not be equated. The devious manoeuvre to hedge this issue, in the Wolf Man case, by suggesting that the wolf-dream at age four had re-cathected with word-representations the thing-representations of the primal scene at age one and a half, thus making it available for thought and anxiety, could not really seal off the problem. Clearly there was an extensive period of early childhood which was not repressed but could nonetheless not be recalled. And clearly there was a vast amount of mental activity going on all the time to which the 'organ for the perception of psychic qualities', consciousness, was simply paying no attention.

It became necessary to consider that the unconscious was too vast and multifacetted a realm of mental activity to be contained in the fragile concept of the 'repressed'. Also called into question was the early imputation from the seventh chapter of *The Interpretation of Dreams*, and the later formulation of the 'Two principles of mental functioning', that the processes in the unconscious were of an inferior order: being among other things timeless, illogical, subject to condensations and displacements, and lacking in negative ideas; this was all placed in doubt by such things as the recognition that dreams and sleep could be thoughtfull and problem-solving. Freud cites the example of mathematical problems being solved during sleep. The trouble lay partly in his attitude toward the dream itself: which considered its function in life to be such a narrow and defensive one – the guardian of sleep. Already the problem of traumatic dreams had contributed (along with the phenomenon of masochism) to the necessity of revising his basic idea of the economic, or quantitative, aspects of mental life; and had led to the formulation in 'Beyond the pleasure principle' of the repetition compulsion as an economic principle more primitive than the pleasure principle. But he was uncertain as to its point of impact. In 'The ego and the id', the problem seems to be bypassed in favour of a new idea: that of fusion and defusion of the two instincts, to account for the para-doxical aspects of instinct life – a move which is on the whole not successful. In general it would seem that the idea that the repeti-tion compulsion can be so powerful that it overrides the pleasure principle and produces phenomena of the ego persevering in a painful position, is a more powerful explanation than the idea that fusions of love and hate – whereby the latter is neutralized in its virulence – come apart and liberate 'pure culture of the death instinct' (as in melancholia).

Probably much of the difficulty of formulation lay in the fact that Freud still lacked a theory of affects, even though his clinical material provides unmistakeable evidence for his deal-ing deeply and sensitively with the emotional relationships of his patients in the consulting room. It is probably the most important – though far from the most obvious – way in which Freud's clinging to the neurophysiological and hydrostatic view of mental life of the *Project*, interfered with the formulation of a satisfactory theory for describing and partially explaining the very complicated phenomena of the transference process. The concept of 'quantities of excitation' as a basis for pleasure and unpleasure, left unformulated the whole area of mental pain; and tended strongly towards a view of life which was essentially denuded of meaning, or rather of meaningfulness. Accordingly, we find Freud returning to the idea of castration anxiety as the central pain; which leaves him in the lurch in cases where exter-nal threats cannot be demonstrated, throwing him back on vague phyllogenetic explanations. Also, of course, it leaves his approach to an understanding of female sexuality unconvincing, to say the least; and imposes on all his formulations the stamp of masculine arrogance, with the female sex taking on the significance of the second-class, *faute de mieux*.

This weakness then finds particular expression in 'The ego and the id', when Freud comes to a definitive clarification of a structural hypothesis for the mental apparatus; dividing its functions into id, ego and superego (or/and ego ideal). While he is able to make a definitive step forward in describing the Oedipus complex in its 'complete' form – as consisting of both masculine and feminine conflicts for each individual – he is still left with terms like 'positive' and 'negative', 'direct' and 'inverted' with their penumbra of value judgment. Consequently, as in the case of the Wolf Man, the 'Case of homosexuality in a woman', and in Schreber or Leonardo, the man's femininity and the woman's masculinity retain their connection with the term 'homosexual'; in spite of his saying in many places that it is a complex and multifacetted term (much like his confused definition of 'unconscious'); it tends to generate confusion rather than clarification. Furthermore, there are attempts to describe the superego in its complete form as derived from 'the forming of a precipitate in the ego, consisting of these two identifications': that is, with both the mother and the father; but despite this, his consideration of the functions of the superego *vis à vis* the ego keeps returning to the father's figure as the central one, as the source of both the 'categorical imperative' of 'thou shalt' and the prohibitive influence of 'thou shalt not'. In the fascinating section on the 'ego's dependent relationships' with id, superego and external reality, Freud comes to take stock of the significance of his theory in its broad outline. And here he is forced in all honesty to recognize that he has put forward a picture of mental life which is pessimistic in the extreme. This will later find definitive expression in *Future of an Illusion, Civilization and its Discontents*, and 'Analysis terminable and interminable'. But the implication is unmistakeable already in 1923 and is very different from the Victorian optimism with which Freud had entered the arena thirty years earlier. The ego is seen here as a poor creature indeed, 'serving three masters', despite its relation to the id having been likened to that of a rider to his horse. Truly a horse may sometimes get the bit in its teeth; sometimes it must be allowed to go the way it prefers; its superior strength must be respected and its dangerousness acknowledged; but one can hardly say overall that the horse is the master. Likewise Freud has made it clear that the ego, through its use of thought as trial action and by means of its exclusive access to the motor apparatus, is able to transform external reality to suit itself – within limits, of course. And finally he describes the superego as having evolved from a specialized function of the ego, through the introjection of the parental figures, just as the ego arose from the id through the exercise of its special perceptual capacities. A paradox is therefore created by the suggestion that it is 'higher' in the evolutionary sense, and derivative from the parental figures, who serve the helplessness of the child with their superior knowledge and strength. How can it be higher and nurturing in origin but a tyrannical master in fact? Here again one feels that preconception has interfered with learning from experience in the theoretical area of Freud's work, for he clings to the formulation that conscience is derived from the 'dissolution of the (genital) Oedipus complex', coincides with the onset of the latency period. Moreover, it is virtually absent in the little girl, who is seen to remain bound to her external objects and be influenced more by fear of the loss of love than by castration anxiety like the little boy, by virtue of her sense of organ inferiority.

How then are we to understand this pessimism? Our concern here is not with how it may be viewed in the context of Freud's personality, his struggles and relationships. I mean rather: how are we to understand the evolution of his ideas so as to comprehend the position that he has reached by 1923? Why is he disposed to view the ego as being so weak, and forced to employ all manner of deceptions like a politician? How is it that these 30 years of work have for virtually the first time produced for psychoanalytical consideration the question: 'How does a person remain well?', in displacement of Freud's constant preoccupation with the problem of the 'choice of neurosis'?

It is striking that no sooner does he ask the question, than he finds in a stroke of astonishing brilliance, the answer which has guided future generations of analysts: though he only formulated the answer clearly, fourteen years later (and it was only applied 23 years later, by Melanie Klein). Only a few months after the publication of 'The ego and the id' he could write in the paper on

'Neurosis and psychosis', speaking of situations of conflict from which the ego must emerge in order to avoid falling ill:

> In the first place the outcome of all such situations will undoubtedly depend on economic considerations - on the relative magnitudes of the trends which are struggling with one another. In the second place it will be possible for the ego to avoid a rupture in any direction by deforming itself, by submitting to encroachments on its own unity and even perhaps by effecting a cleavage or division of itself. In this way the inconsistencies, eccentricities and follies of men would appear in a similar light to their sexual perversions, through the acceptance of which they spare themselves repressions. (p. 152)

Other aspects of the answer to the question of the sources of the pessimism inherent in Freud's theoretical construction at this time, may be found in two conceptions which he has touched upon but not yet utilized. The first of these is the quality of omnipotence, which he had clearly recognized in the clinical phenomena of the Rat Man, the Wolf Man, and Schreber. The second is the formulation of an 'internal world' or 'world of phantasy'. This played a large part in the understanding of Schreber's 'world destruction phantasy', and there Freud realized that it could be considered that the 'world' which fell to destruction from the withdrawal of libido from objects, had been composed of the 'sum total of sublimations and identifications' which made up the foundations of character. But he could not find a substantial place for it in his structural theory of the mind because he could not ascribe to it a constructive significance. In 1924, in the paper 'The loss of reality in neurosis and psychosis', he writes:

> The sharp distinction between neurosis and psychosis, however, is weakened by the circumstance that in neurosis too there is no lack of attempts to replace a disagreeable reality by one which is more in keeping with the subject's wishes. This is made possible by the existence of a world of phantasy, of a domain which becomes separated from the real external work at the time of the introduction of the reality principle. This domain has since been kept free from the demands of the exigencies of life, like a kind of 'reservation'. (p. 187)

By this time he had returned the function of reality testing (earlier ascribed to the ego ideal) to the list of the ego's tasks and capabilities.

In bringing to a close this consideration of 'The ego and the id' and taking stock of the position which Freud had reached in his attempts to formulate conceptual equipment for describing (and in some measure explaining) the phenomenology of his consulting room, I suggest that one should bear in mind for future consideration, the defects in his approach. Firstly, he had no adequate theory of affects, and was still thinking of quantities of excitation. Secondly, the loci of conflict had not yet been pinpointed, partly because he was still inclined to a unitary hypothesis in this area. Thirdly, he had failed to make use of the attribute of omnipotence of which he had found abundant evidence. Fourthly, he was still inclined to attribute a trivial function to the dream as the guardian of sleep. And finally, he was disinclined to see in the 'world of phantasy' an aspect of the 'world' of the mind that had a reality of its own which rivalled in significance the reality with which the external world was apprehended.

CHAPTER FOURTEEN

The last years (anxiety and the economics of the mind)

We come now to the rather sad last years of Freud's life: the last twelve years from the writing of 'Inhibition, symptom and anxiety' until his death. For despite being ill he seems to have worked a lot: in between a dozen operations he wrote three volumes of papers. His interest certainly turned very strongly toward retrospection on the implications of psychoanalytic findings for other fields – anthropology, sociology, and politics; and he produced these works: *The Future of an Illusion, Civilization and its Discontents,* and *Moses and Monotheism*, which I personally do not find very interesting. There is a change in his style of writing: it becomes very prolix and diffuse in many places; I think writing had probably become a necessary part of his life, and of course the people who followed him were interested in anything written by him.

However, I do not wish to discuss these works; rather, I propose to study the winding-up and tying together of his clinical ideas and the tools and equipment of psychoanalysis – developments in his attitudes rather than his technique: such as the problem of female sexuality; a more definitive view of the perversions; and a clearer shape to the concept of splitting of the ego and the mechanisms of psychopathology. All this makes a substantial though not perhaps a major contribution, such as occurred throughout the marvellous six years from 1920 to 1926, in which the whole theory was revised to become the Structural Theory, and with it the model of the mind for use in the consulting room. 'Inhibition, symptom and anxiety', or 'The problem of anxiety' as it is sometimes called, really reversed Freud's previous stand concerning anxiety. He tended earlier to consider it to be a kind of noise made in the mind as a result of the stagnation of sexual impulses and their transformation into mental pain. But here he decides that anxiety is really at the heart of the matter, and he uses the term not simply as a descriptive one (as previously), but as a general term for the kind of mental pain that functions as a signal of some impending disorder in the mind. This signal theory of anxiety is the one with which we actually work; although of course the theory of anxiety has undergone a considerable change in the hands of Mrs Klein, though her division of it into persecutory anxiety (corresponding to Freud's signal) and depressive anxieties, which corresponds more to a concept of mental pain.

In this way Freud came gradually to consider that the problems with which psychoanalysis was concerned were best stated in terms more closely related to the concept of affects. He seemed to come around to the view that affects and particularly painful affects, were at the heart of the matter; and that the pleasure principle was not simply a matter of avoiding unpleasure, but was really a matter of dealing with mental pain of various sorts. This really fitted in place the ultimate piece necessary for a workable model of the mind: one which, I think, has remained the model which we use in psychoanalysis. The structure of the mind – the ego, superego and id – has been only slightly modified through the tendency to think more of 'self ' than of ego and id: that is, to think of self as being composed of ego and id and split in various ways. Essentially, we still think of it as ego and id in its origins, but as 'self' operationally. There is great beauty in Freud's idea that the primordial personality, the primordial mind, was originally all id, and that out of it evolved a separate organ of the mind – the ego – from the impact of experience; and that from this evolved the superego, as a result of introjective and other processes. His evolutionary view of the way in which the development of the mind recapitulates the evolution of mind in the species, has remained a happy model which most analysts find inspiring rather than useful.

In the years which followed the establishment of this model of the mind, Freud was very ill, and also very preoccupied with the applications of psychoanalytic thought; trying to understand what the psychoanalytic movement signified in the world. But he still continued to do clinical work and certainly a tremendous amount of supervision of his colleagues. By this time he was fairly convinced that the limitations of an analyst's work were imposed mainly by the degree to which he had made contact with his own unconscious 'complexes' (as he still called them): by his unconscious conflict. But he had also realized very astutely that an analyst's work was dependent on continuation of the self-analytic process in the course of his work and of his daily life. He was also forced by various tragedies to realize that analysis, like most professions, or most jobs, carries an industrial hazard: analytic work was seen to be a danger to the analyst's mental health. And at this time he advised analysts to go back to analysis every five years. The training analysis at that time was a very cursory affair indeed, however; Freud (in about 1935) was think-ing of it as something lasting only a few months, which was to be mainly devoted to the analyst getting a first-hand experience of the analytic method at work, and learning the rudiments of dream analysis and introspection. It was better than the walks in the park he had had with Ferenczi; but it was not a therapeutic view of the training analysis, which only grew up in the years following his death, when the third generation of analysts were to be trained. Freud was very specific himself, particularly in the paper 'Analysis terminable and interminable', that there is no complete analysis: that any analysis is, at its best, a preparation for a continuation of selfscrutiny and development, and it is not meant to protect people from having conflicts in life, but only to equip them to meet these. Analysis is the beginning, and not the end, of a process.

His interest in psychopathology lessened considerably during this time, it seems to me; and his interest in healthy development increased in two directions. The first is manifest in his chang-ing views about female sexuality. The realization grew upon him that women analysts were able to get a different view of female sexuality, not just by virtue of being women and knowing at first-hand, but also because they elicited a richer maternal transference from their patients. This was true at that time, when male analysts did not know how to pick up the phenomenology of the maternal transference so well, and tended to work very much in the so-called 'father complex', recognizing mainly the paternal transference. Freud acknowledged his indebtedness to the women analysts of that era, and the changes in his views on female sexuality were I think very salutary ones; he partly gave up the differentiation of active and passive as if it were equivalent to masculine and feminine, and recognized the strong active trends that are present in femininity as well as in masculinity. This went a little distance toward the recognition of passivity as a more pathological phenomenon, to be differentiated from dependence and receptivity. He did rather cling to the view that the little girl knew nothing of her vagina and had no vaginal sensations, although he acknowledges that women may know more about this and that here he might be wrong. He also acknowledged that perhaps his view that women's primary difficulty stems from penis envy was an exaggerated one; and that their penis envy (as Helene Deutsch and others insisted) might be a very secondary thing, not at all the primary manifestation of emerging femininity. Most importantly, he became aware that the little girl has a terrific task on her hands in forming her Oedipus complex – that is, her feminine Oedipus complex. Because the difficulty of changing from her primary pregenital (which he still insists on calling 'pre-oedipal') attachment was so great, the formation of a strong oedipal attachment to the father was a much heavier task than the little boy's sexualization of his primary relationship to his mother in his masculine Oedipus complex. He devotes a lot of thought to how it is the little girl manages this; and when he lists motives which may drive her in this direction, they are primarily grievances against the mother: that the mother did not give her a penis, that the mother provided her with sexual stimulation while changing her nappies but did not give her full satisfaction; envy of the mother, castration anxiety and the belief that she has been castrated at the mother's hands, anxiety about being devoured by the mother, are all based on careful clinical observation. But it is all rather negative motivation, propelled by grievances on the one hand and anxieties on the other, and generally conducive of a picture of femininity as a rather unwholesome affair. What it lacks, and what is missing generally from his theoretical views in these later years, is really a use of the concept of identification. That is, he does not allow sufficiently for the little girl's positive motivation of identification with her mother, through which she may turn to her father in a loving way via the mother's love for the father. Therefore he cannot allow for the intensity of the little girl's longing for babies from the father; but thinks primarily of her craving sexual gratification on the one hand, or the various motives for revenge on the mother for disappointments, on the other. Although the view of female sexuality makes a big step forward in acknowledging the complexity and the role of activity, paying a tribute to the difficulty of the task of the little girl, it does not quite grasp the positive and tender motivation in her. Freud implies on the contrary that she is drawn to the father and to the penis, as the object of sexual desire, from primarily spiteful and negative motives. He speaks of little girls' attachment to their dolls, but tends to view this only as some sort of competition with the mother, and does not take into account admiration for the mother and the positive aspects of identification which play a role in the formation of the little girl's Oedipus complex.

Probably Freud had forgotten along the way the ego-ideal aspects of the superego: those aspects of encouragement and nurturing and fostering which the superego maintains toward the ego. I think there is no doubt that his views about severity of the superego hardened during this time, affecting his idea of the therapeutic task in analysis to the extent that he states quite unequivocally that part of the therapeutic task is to free the ego from the domination of the superego. In later psychoanalysts' writing, this is modified so that Freud's phrase 'the dissolution of the Oedipus complex' becomes 'the dissolution of the superego'. This reminds one of the joke that the superego is the alcohol-soluble fraction of the personality – a wry joke indeed.

This would place psychoanalysis in a position to promulgate a value system devoted entirely to cultural adaptation, leaving no room for individual development and individuality or idiosyncrasy in values, for independence of one's culture and a healthy kind of rebelliousness. It is mainly from this point of view that Freud's late attitude toward the psychoanalytical method and its efficacy was pessimistic; and this pessimism is most clearly brought out in the famous paper 'Analysis terminable and interminable'. This attitude left the ego with no ego ideal relationship to the superego; it did not allow the superego any function of promoting ideals and values and, in the absence of any internal source of ideals and values, these would really have to be absorbed from the external culture. This is related to the whole trend in *Civilization and its Discontents* to the effect that adaptation to the culture is a necessity and that it is achieved at the expense of internal freedom. He does not conceive the possibility of freedom and a healthy maladaptation to a bad culture.

I suggest that the pessimism about analysis that percolates through 'Analysis terminable and interminable' is of a very peculiar sort. It seems to me that it is an outgrowth of Freud thinking of the analytical method and analytical theories as if they were complete (although he would absolutely deny this in theory); as if the method had now been brought to its perfection, and its efficacy could be evaluated in some final way. The weight comes down very much on the side of what psychoanalysis cannot do, because of the 'quantitative' or 'economic' factors. These economic factors were felt to be connected with the death instinct and destructiveness (primary sadism, primary masochism, secondary sadism and masochism); and the strength of these impulses was felt to create the negative therapeutic reaction in analysis. It manifest itself as what he called 'inertia' or 'stickiness' in the transference, and created the opposition to cure and the clinging to guilt. These three link together: the stickiness or the inertia of the libido as it is manifest in the transference; the tendency to negative therapeutic reaction to any step forward in insight; and the factor of the patient clinging, rather masochistically, to the repetition of his experiences of guilt.

One cannot escape the impression that he had had himself, and saw his colleagues having repeatedly, experiences of analyses grinding to a halt, long before a really satisfactory therapeutic result had been achieved. Freud considered these factors to be mainly constitutional; modified of course by the experience of the first five years of life which he considered to be so absolutely crucial. After these first five years, very little, if any, effect on personality structure could be expected. By the time the latency period was established, the personality structure and the fundamentals of character were likewise established. The implications of that paper had a rather bad effect on the development of analysis. First of all, they tended to discourage character analysis; secondly, they tended to encourage analysts to restrict themselves to curing symptoms; and thirdly through the tone of the paper, to discourage technical innovation or experimentation. Freud had already spoken quite harshly of the experiments that Ferenczi had made in his last years with more active techniques; of other attempts to shorten the process; and of technical methods for dealing with resistances other than by interpretation. His attitude toward child analysis (although in two footnotes he gives credit to its developers) dismissed it from playing a serious role in the future of psychoanalysis from either the social or the scientific point of view. This, I think, probably relates back to the relatively small yield that he drew from Little Hans: that case, in all its richness, was after all used almost exclusively to corroborate the evidence already drawn from adult analysis for the existence of the infantile neurosis and the reality of the Oedipus complex.

In many ways Freud was right; but not for the right reasons. He was right because it has turned out that child analysis is so difficult, that not many people can do it well, that not many people who do it well can do it for many years, and that parents are not willing to make the sacrifices that are necessary for extensive analysis of children. The tendency is certainly for child analysis to gravitate to the child guidance clinics and into the hands of young people with low scientific status, too low for research accomplishment. I think it never occurred to Freud that the psychoanalysis of children would bring innovations to the technical aspects of the psychoanalysis of adult patients.

Finally there is another possible reason which may contribute to the pessimism of 'Analysis terminable and interminable', one probably more personal to Freud. Perhaps he was disappointed in the quality of people who were attracted to psychoanalytical work, whereas in the very early years, his optimism and enthusiasm had tended to cause him to idealize the people who gathered around him. Disillusion ensued when he discovered that naturally the people who were drawn to psychoanalysis were, by and large, people who needed psychoanalytical treatment. Because psycho-analysis was still in its early stages and its therapeutic efficacy was limited, it could not be expected to have the degree of success that would enable its students to do first class psychoanalyti-cal work, or to withstand the industrial hazard. This pessimism was an outgrowth of Freud's tendency to view the method and technique as being far advanced, rather than rudimentary and in its infancy as a science. For instance, he always thought that psychotic illnesses and psychotic aspects of the personality would remain outside the possibility of psychoanalytic influence: such patients would be unable to form a transference neurosis. A transference psychosis of the Wolf Man's 1926 illness does not seem to have altered his view.

Because the psychoses drew their origins from such an early pre-verbal period in the history of the individual, so as to be beyond the possibility of recall, Freud was unable to formulate a therapeutic process comparable with recovery from the infan-tile amnesia. This brings us to another paper very closely tied to 'Analysis terminable and interminable': namely the little paper on 'Constructions in analysis' – by which he meant what we would call 'reconstructions in analysis'. Here it is quite clear that his view of the analytical method still treated it as something of a jigsaw puzzle. Interpretation certainly is seen as a moment-to-moment activity of the analyst dealing with the bits of material as they come along; but the important and synthetic work of the analyst is considered to be the creation of the reconstruction of the history of the infantile neurosis, which the analyst then has to 'work through' gradually to enable the patient to accept and be influenced by it. Freud felt that the therapeutic task was very dependent on this intellectual activity of the analyst and the intellectual acceptance of it by the patient; for this reconstruction was supposed to assist in the relief of the infantile amnesia and the recovery of sufficient memories of the period of the infantile neurosis, to be convincing to the patient.

The very earliest year of life or earliest eighteen months prior to the development of the capacity to verbalize, did not allow the thing-representations to become word-representations which could become accessible to consciousness. Freud was in this way hamstrung by his own theories about how the mind worked; he could not conceive of the possibility that remembering could take place in action, simply as transference experience. This is partly because his idea of the truth continued to refer to the knowledge of external reality; which in turn may be seen as the consequence of his never fully conceptualizing (in spite of using the phrase 'internal world') a space in the mind occupied by figures of continuous existence, rather than by 'imagos'. And because his idea of an internal world never reached beyond this, his concept of truth could not become one of the knowledge of psychic reality; despite his calling consciousness an 'organ for the perception of psychic qualities'. The accomplishment of a sense of reality, and the achievement of mental health, meant to him specifically the elimination of the tendency to infantile transference distortion: that is, the tendency of the past to distort perception and experience of the outside world in the present. This seems to me to have placed a very great limitation on his thought about the nature of mental health.

On the other hand he made a great step forward during these years in coming to think about mental health as a problem for psychoanalysis to investigate as a thing in itself, not merely as the absence or negative of psychopathology. In two papers – that on 'Fetishism' and that on 'The splitting of the ego in the service of defence' – he does raise the question of how a person may remain healthy, and he immediately answers it in a very brilliant way. He suggests that the person achieves it by splitting his ego and relegating the less healthy parts of his ego to repressions, to being encapsulated by defences in some manner; and the healthy part of his ego, he turns towards the outside world. In arriving at this concept of splitting of the ego in relation to fetishism, and then applying it to the question of how a person remains healthy, Freud did provide an answer of a most useful nature. But it would be incorrect to assume that this is the same use of the term 'splitting processes' as that employed by Melanie Klein in her 1946 paper. There, she describes splitting processes as a 'schizoid mechanism'; she means an entirely different thing from Freud. Freud referred primarily to a splitting of the attention, which thus brought about some sort of division in the ego; attention to the outside world could be carried on by the healthy part, and attention to symptoms and to superego could be carried on by those parts of the personality afflicted by psychopathological formations. Previously he had assumed that the ego was a single synthetic organ of the mind; and in spite of all the evidence to the contrary (with Schreber, for instance) he never systematically questioned this, until he considered reformulating fetishism.

I will now summarize the development in these last years from the point of view of clinical psychoanalysis. It is important to understand the pessimism which afflicts these years somewhat, since it has had an immense influence in various ways on the development of psychoanalytic thought. This influence has consisted primarily in encouraging orthodoxy; in discouraging technical innovation; and tending to preserve to some degree the energetics concept of the Libido Theory, infusing this a little into the Structural Theory of the mind. For Freud himself preserved in this way his own preoccupation with with the quantitative aspects of things. I think that this category of metapsychology (the economic category: the preoccupation with the quantitative relationships) is without doubt theoretically correct; but is practically quite useless, and tends to serve for analysts the function of an escape-hatch or rubbish-bin into which analytic failures may be dumped. It discourages a more pugnacious attitude toward analytical failures; dissuades the analyst from full responsibility for his own failures; and encourages a tendency to blame the patient and assume that the failure of an analysis is that of the patient and not of the analyst. One of the unsavoury manifestations is the emergence of the term 'unanalysable', which comprises a sort of political conviction, a relegation to a psychoanalytical Siberia. This seems to me to have arisen in direct relation to the paper 'Analysis terminable and interminable', and to be the most unfortunate part of the legacy that we have received from Freud, glorious as it is in other ways.